D1880052

The Spirit and Spirituality of Kailas and Manasarovar

The Spirit and Spirituality of Kailas and Manasarovar

Dr. Taradatt

GYAN

© **Author**

All rights reserved. No part of this work may be reproduced, stored, adapted, or transmitted in any form or by any means, electronic, mechanical, photocopying, micro-filming, recording or otherwise, or translated in any language, without the prior written permission of the copyright owner and the publisher. The book is sold subject to the condition that it shall not, by way of trade or otherwise, be lent, resold, hired out, or otherwise circulated without the prior publisher's written consent in any form of binding or cover other than that in which it is published.

The views and opinions expressed in this book are author's own and the facts reported by him have been verified to the extent possible, and the publishers are not in any way liable for the same. Some of the images have been taken from the web based open sources and acknowledged to the extent possible.

Published, 2021

Published by

Gyan Publishing House
5, Ansari Road
Daryaganj, New Delhi-110002
Phone: 011-47034999, 9811692060
www.gyanbooks.com
E-mail: books@gyanbooks.com

Printed at: Gyan Press, Delhi.

Cataloging in Publication Data—DK
Courtesy: D.K. Agencies (P) Ltd. <docinfo@dkagencies.com>

Taradatt, 1956- author.
The spirit and spirituality of Kailas and Manasarovar / Dr. Taradatt. — Edition first.
pages cm
ISBN: 9788121220194 (HB)

1. Kailas, Mount (China)—Description and travel. 2. Manasarowar Lake (China)—Description and travel. 3. Kailas, Mount (China)—Guidebooks. 4. Manasarowar Lake (China)—Guidebooks. 5. Hindu pilgrims and pilgrimages—China—Kailas, Mount. 6. Hindu pilgrims and pilgrimages—China—Manasarowar Lake. 7. Taradatt, 1956- —Travel—China—Kailas, Mount. 8. Taradatt, 1956- —Travel—China—Manasarowar Lake. I. Title.

LCC DS786.T37 2021 | DDC 915.1504 23

In Memory of My Brother
Late Shri S.N. Pathak

Contents

Preface

Kailas and Manasarovar were folklore and woven into almost every tale I heard during my childhood from my parents and village elders. It was not uncommon to be reverentially told about long and arduous journeys undertaken in the then not-too-distant past by saints and devotees of Lord Shiva from the village environs to the sacred Mount Kailas and Lake Manasarovar. The sub-text was their die-hard spirit amidst adverse climatic conditions, inadequate information, and lack of material resources. The distance was hardly ever perceived to be a constraint. There were also multiple access points and routes through the mighty Himalayas to enter Tibet where Kailas and Manasarovar were situated. Societal and trading ties with Tibet were strong. Barter of edibles and other consumer goods was common in the mutual interests of people living on this side of the Himalayas and those on its extensive plateau. Geographical inputs about the two sacred *tirthas* shared by traders from Tibet served as invaluable nuggets of information for pilgrims. But naturally, I grew up excited by thoughts of travelling to the sacred Kailas-Manasarovar some day. My interest transformed into determination soon after I formally studied the ancient scriptures and later on into obstinacy when faced with gross administrative adversities to travel.

Even after India became an independent political unit in the year 1947 and Tibet was recognised as an autonomous region under the People's Republic of China, barter trade with Tibet had continued and pilgrimages to Kailas-

Manasarovar hardly faced restrictions. The situation changed suddenly in the year 1962 when an expansionist regime from the other side of the border invaded its unsuspecting friendly neighbour. The possibility of my visiting Kailas-Manasarovar vaned and every thought of it got relegated to the deep recesses of my mind in spite of curiosity remaining alive.

I was fortunate to get an opportunity to study Sanskrit literature and ancient scriptures, which included mythological texts and metaphysics of various religions. Naturally, my interest in the spirit and spirituality of Kailas-Manasarovar stood re-kindled to a higher dimension even though a journey once imagined had no scope of materialising.

The door for Kailas-Manasarovar reopened in the year 1981. It was thus now possible for Indians to pay a visit to these holy places albeit in very limited numbers. Every year since then, the Ministry of External Affairs provides assistance, on self-financing basis, to selected Yatris undertaking the Kailas Manasarovar Yatra (KMY) via the 5,335 metre (17,500 feet) high Lipulekh Pass connecting Uttarakhand with Tibet by providing facilities like transportation, accommodation, food, medical tests, guides, etc. Besides various Indian agencies, the Ministry also coordinates with the Government of Peoples' Republic of China for the smooth conduct of this Yatra. The Yatra has been quite recently enhanced to 18 batches of a maximum of 60 Yatris per batch. Each batch is coordinated and led by a Government-sponsored Liaison Officer.

I, thus, made my first attempt to join one such batch of Central Government-sponsored pilgrims in 1996. After having joined the Indian Administrative Service (IAS) in 1983, I was then working as Director, Agriculture and Food Production in the State Government of Odisha. To my bad luck, my application was summarily rejected by the State

Government on the ground that nothing worthwhile would be achieved. I could not pass the first hurdle to even reach the selection process of Union Ministry of External Affairs for consideration of my candidature. It was of no consequence to the decision-taker that I had sought permission to undertake the journey in my private capacity and at personal expense. The relevant rules clearly permit All Indian Service officers to avail of duty leave for it.

In the year 2003 after seeing the advertisement of the Yatra by Ministry of External Affairs, while working as Director in the Central Ministry of Home Affairs I applied, cautiously requesting consideration of my candidature as a Liaison Officer or a common pilgrim. Selection of Liaison Officer was to be done through an interview and that of general candidates through a lottery system. I was called for the interview, when I informed the panel of authorized senior officers of Ministry of External Affairs of my desire to write a book on the basis of my study of ancient literature and the reality to be experienced during the actual Yatra. My track record of trekking, upbringing in the high Himalayan mountain ranges, interest and study of ancient scriptures and travel curiosity all proved inutile. I was disappointed not to figure in the select list of Liaison Officers nor of Yatris. However, there was no question of losing heart.

I made a third attempt in the year 2005 with greater determination, when my Central tenure as Joint Secretary, Ministry of Health & Family Welfare was coming to an end. As on the previous occasion, my interactions during the interview gave me hope, but only to be frustrated yet again.

This time, I was in no mood to miss the opportunity of visiting Kailas-Manasarovar. A travel agent offered to fulfil my long-cherished desire instantly by travelling via

Kathmandu, Nepal. I took a month-long leave from office. My long-awaited pilgrimage was a blissful experience in more ways than one; the journey included another high point – darshan of Pasupathi Nath at his temple in Kathmandu.

But naturally, my yearning to go there through the traditional route in Uttarakhand remained undiminished. Besides reliving my boyhood amidst the immense natural beauty of the high Himalayan ranges, a principal reason was to see the places mentioned in mythological texts written in Sanskrit. It was also becoming difficult to act upon my plan of writing a book on the subject without visiting them. Besides the *Ramayana* of Sage Valmiki and *Mahabharata* of Sage Vyasa, the *Manas Khand* of *Skanda Purana*, in particular, contains vivid descriptions of Kailas-Manasarovar and holy places en-route, mostly in Kumaon region, and onward into Tibet from Lipulekh Pass. The KMY steered each year by Ministry of External Affairs alone could suffice to meet my needs. I thus ventured to apply for the fourth time in the year 2014 to participate as a common pilgrim, showing no ambition to secure the prestigious Liaison Officer's selection. Unlike earlier, the State Government of Odisha did not question the utility of my travel and conveyed its no objection by forwarding my application. My name figured in the 'Waiting List' announced by Ministry of External Affairs, but that became meaningless at the end.

In true die-hard spirit, I applied the following year. This time I got selected. I was selected in the precious first batch of pilgrims, and thus undertook my long-cherished venture in June 2015. I was quite intrigued to hear from some fellow Yatris that they had performed the same Yatra in batches of their choice with their friends many times in past. There is no point in venturing into factors leading to selection of well-connected candidates.

It may be inappropriate to say that this book is an exhaustive account of my pilgrimage to Kailas-Manasarovar which may help or guide future pilgrims convincingly. It would be equally an exaggeration to claim that it contains exhaustive references of all the holy places en-route or in relation to references to Kailas-Manasarovar in ancient scriptures and in any other forms of literary expressions. Indeed, soon after performing the Yatra, when I was carrying out a literature review before penning my book, I got to read the unique magnum opus "*Kailas-Manasarovar*" by the renowned sage and geographer, Swami Pranavanand published in the year 1949. This great treatise overwhelmed me as it contained materials far more than I could think of, and my resolve to continue my project wavered whenever I reflected on what my contributions to the subject could be.

My life took an unexpected turn in March 2016 when my elder brother and a treasured guide throughout my life left our family for his heavenly abode all of a sudden. In a state of deep shock for some time, I was reminded of my promise to him to write a book on Kailas-Manasarovar. His memory pervading all thoughts; my promise haunted me daily. I decided to pay my homage to him on the occasion of his first death anniversary by delivering on my words to him. A few months after his demise, I had superannuated after serving for 33 years in the IAS. Giving myself an almost impossible timeline, this book written then in Hindi became the result of my intensive but hurried efforts.

This book elaborates on that effort and contains narratives found in ancient scriptures in relation to Kailas-Manasarovar and important places en-route the Yatra via Lipulekh Pass. I am sure those interested in the subject would be benefitted from references to mythology and poetry uniquely cited herein from age-old Sanskrit texts, which are largely found missing in books written in recent times by travellers and authors. I draw upon different shades of spirituality and the spirit of the sacred Mount and Lake, to Hindus, Jains and Bon (indigenous religion traditional to Tibet), and surroundings of Buddhist influences.

In writing the script, I was aware that what I was to offer the reader had to go beyond what is already mentioned widely across the rich ancient texts and in some books written by modern Indian and Western authors. My contribution is thus to also put together selectively and analytically what may have been stated in a different context across various books.

I have referred to books written by old pilgrims also. In particular, I would like to mention two books which have been used extensively, coincidently both similarly titled– "*Kailas and Manasarovar*". The 1949 magnum opus of Swami Pranavanand I have already drawn attention to earlier. The other is by late Shri Sushil Kumar Bhattacharya, originally written in Bangla, the translation of which in Hindi was published in 1939. While Swami Pranavananda's "*Kailas-Manasarovar*" includes results of deeper scientific and academic studies he had undertaken over a long period of time, Sushil Kumar Bhattacharya wrote an interesting travelogue after his long and arduous pilgrimage with a band of friends. I have also gained valuable insights from the book "*Paramapoojya Sri Narayan Swami Evam Sri Narayan Ashram*" (*परम पूज्य श्री नारायण स्वामी एवं श्री नारायण आश्रम*), written by Smt. Draupadi Garbyal.

Although the reader will find narratives around places en-route KMY, these do not necessarily follow the sequence of places usually visited during the Yatra. I have attempted to elaborate and correlate a few sites of sacred geography mentioned in Manas Khand of Skanda Purana, which figure along this route. These could help shape and enrich the overall experience of inquisitive pilgrims and tourists. For the passionate traveller, I have also drawn out a few memories, photographs and shared stories from various published works such as "*Kailas Yatra*" by Kevin Bubriski and Abhimanyu Pandey, International Centre for Integrated Mountain Development (ICIMOD), and by travel writer Colin Thubron who discusses spirituality, religion, and sorrow in his book "*To a Mountain in Tibet*".

The KMY starts from the national capital, New Delhi, and takes about three weeks to be completed. My batch had night halts at Almora, Dharchula, Sirakha, Gala, Budhi, Gunji and Nabhidang on the Indian side, and at Taklakot, Darchen, Driraphuk, Junjhu-Pu/Jong Jerbu, and Kyugu in Tibet. Yatris got one extra day for acclimatization at Gunji before crossing through Lipulekh Pass for entry in Tibet.

About 20 km after crossing the Line of Actual Control (LAC) at Lipulekh Pass, Yatris are transported by Chinese authorities in buses to Taklakot for passport and visa verification and making payments for transportation and other facilities pre-arranged by them for the Yatris. The remaining part of the Yatra, except the *parikramas* (Sanskrit for circumambulation; kora in Tibetan) of Mount Kailas in part and Lake Manasarovar, is performed using this paid-for transport. Road infrastructure created on the Tibetan plateau is impressive. Besides one extra day at Taklakot, two nights and three days spent at Kyugu/Qugu by the side of Lake Manasarovar offer the Yatris much needed rest and opportunity to meditate, explore and enjoy the environment.

At the onset of the return journey from Kailas-Manasarovar, Yatris get an opportunity to visit Purang valley of Tibet, specially the ancient monastery of Khojarnath and Toyo village. The *Samadhi* or memorial of General Zoravar Singh, despite being substantially destroyed during the cultural revolution of China, continues to narrate the tale of the legendary General of Kashmir who had defeated the much stronger local army to hoist the Dogra flag on a substantial part of Tibet. The book contains interesting tales of Khojarnath and General Zoravar Singh in brief.

Yatris are usually afforded opportunity to visit the ancient group of Jageshwar temples and Patal Bhubaneshwar cave in Almora and Pithoragarh districts respectively through small diversions on the route. Religious and socio-cultural significance of these places has been explained briefly in the book in the light of what has been mentioned in ancient scriptures. A brief description of Chaudas and Vyas valleys, including contribution of Sage Narayan Swami, in this book interest those desirous to know about the bordering areas of Kumaon in Uttarakhand.

Government of India keeps reviewing and modifying the KMY duration and route routinely. Indeed, when I had performed the Yatra, the route had already shrunk from about 27 days to 23 days. But, after completion of the strategic roads, until recently under construction in Pithoragarh district bordering Tibet, it is expected that the duration of KMY would be about two weeks. Real adventure and excitement during the pilgrimage, in that case, however, could diminish substantially for many pilgrims, though it might make possible the less-physically arduous travel for some others. I may note that the geographical distance of Kailas and Manasarovar from the Indian border is not much. Indeed, the distance of these two places from Almora district headquarters is about 250 miles; about the same as from Delhi to Almora. The aerial distance is much less.

This book with limited copies was originally published in 2017 in Hindi, and was not available in the open market. Those who helped me in various ways include friends and fellow Yatris. I would like to acknowledge the contributions of Sri Vijoy Daga and Sri Sunil Vavade, in particular, for sharing beautiful photographs of places we visited together during the Yatra. My dear batch mate Dr. KP Krishnan provided thoughtful comments and my knowledgeable friend and former IPS officer Sri AK Upadhyaya shared useful inputs about Mount Kailas. Their contributions are respectfully acknowledged. I thank the publisher for his unstinting support for this book from our very first conversation.

My younger brothers, Nawin, Harish and Bhuwan, have greatly supported me throughout with encouragement and in many invaluable ways. I pray to the Almighty for their well-being and happiness.

Naukuchiatal **Taradatt**
31 October 2020

Images of Kailas and Manasarovar

Kailas, with its surrounding range

Mysterious Kailas, south face

Sacred aura of Kailas, north face

Kailas and Manasarovar: Profound Divinity

Manasarovar during sunrise

Manasarovar: Heaven on Earth

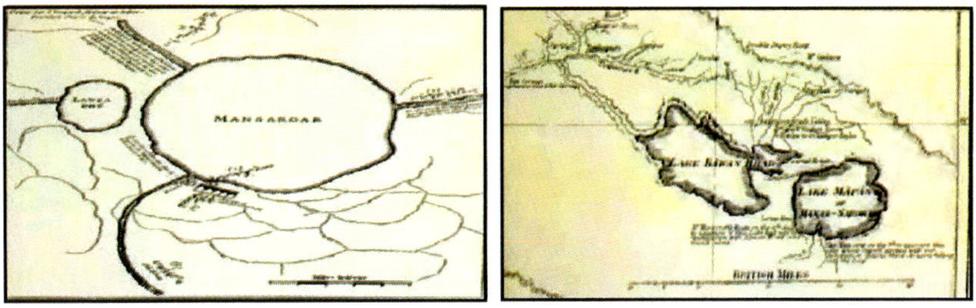

Anquetil du Perron, 1731-1805; William Moorecroft, 1812 (Yatra)

Government of India: Kailas-Manasarovar Yatra Route

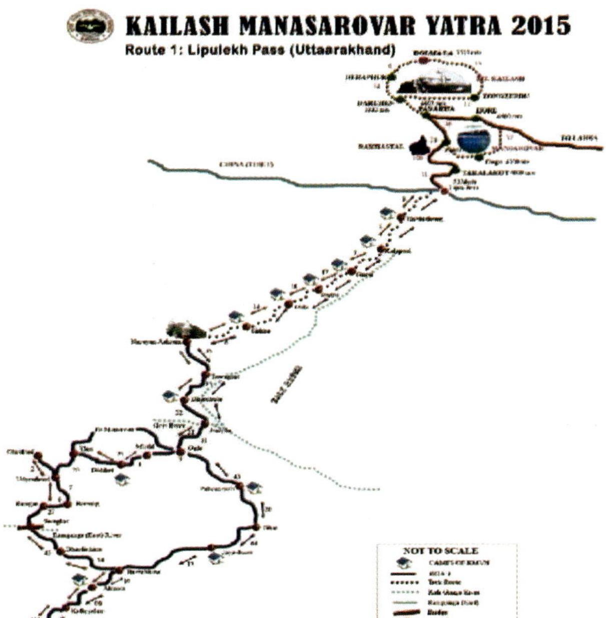

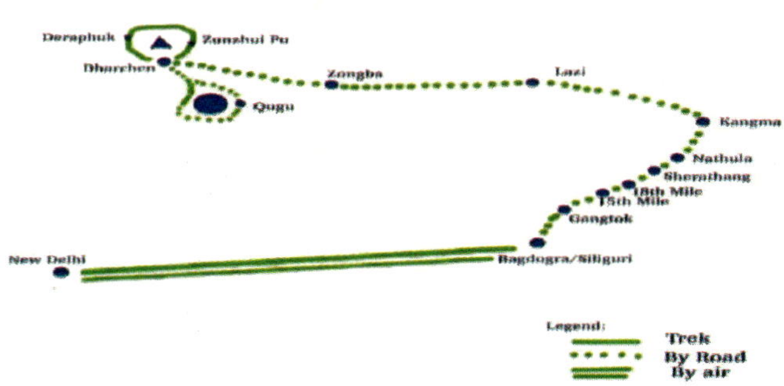

Landmarks Kailas, Manasarovar and Rakshastal Kailas

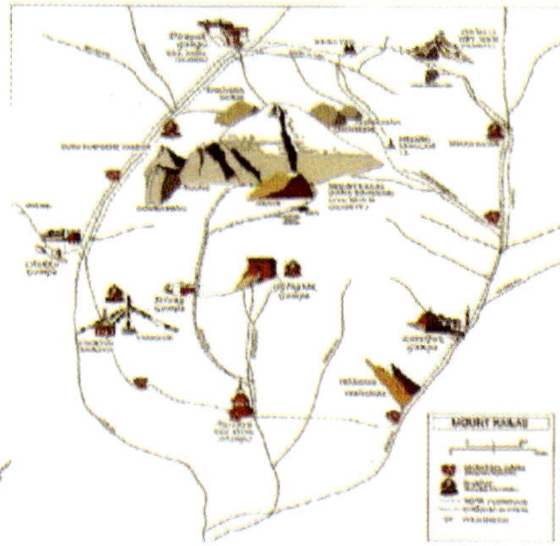

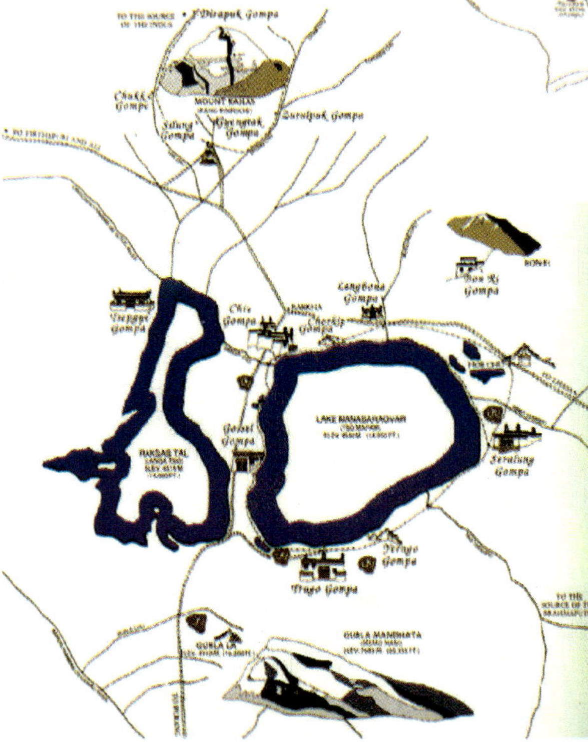

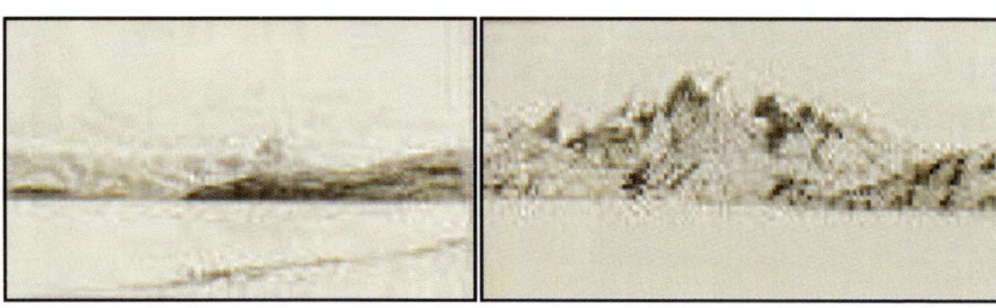

Rakshastal Kailas and Mandhata; Dr. Sven Hedin's "Trans-Himalaya: Discoveries and Adventurers in Tibet, Vol. I", 1909

1

Pilgrimage for tranquillity and transcendental knowledge: Relevance and eligibility

From time immemorial, the objective of human life on this planet has been a mystery - a matter of curiosity and investigation for inquisitive thinkers. Both Eastern and Western philosophers as well as explorers of other hues have been articulating their thoughts and experiences on this issue depending upon their perceptions and predilections from time to time. Philosophical thoughts or the metaphysics of religions written and interpreted in different parts of the world is vast in volume, containing illustrations and in-depth understanding of sages and seers. There is no dearth of academic literature or anecdotal recounting on a variety of religious involvements which have undergone internal and external examinations of followers and critics. Despite differences of opinion in relation to various religions in terms of mythological descriptions, rituals and associated paraphernalia, the deeper and dispassionate internal examinations of yester-year explorers embodied in ancient literature seem to be suggestive of their metaphysical core being the same or similar. None has cared, nor dared, to state with reasoning that it is not the same.

All religions accept the importance of material well-being of the society in its worldly existence. Again, none has reached the conclusion that the gross happiness of material life, which is momentary in this physical world, is the ultimate goal of human existence. Conspicuous consumption may be the principal destination of a capitalist economy, but it can not be concluded to be the ultimate goal of all men. From a metaphysical viewpoint, almost all religions consider either self-realization or realization of the Ultimate Reality, or access to "Heaven" as the final objective of human life.

Ancient Indian tradition known as Vedic or Sanatan Dharma while acknowledging the importance of material attainments for a healthy existence, lays emphasis on disciplined consumption with a slant towards controlled consumer behaviour in lieu of conspicuous indulgences. It unequivocally declares that continuing efforts and material gains despite being essential for worldly enjoyment or sensual pleasure, can never be the ultimate objective of life because this enjoyment is neither absolute nor unending. An exploration driven by greed leading to restlessness or dissatisfaction cannot be considered to be life's ultimate end. Material gains associated with opulence and power, according to Sanatan Dharma, provide transitory rather than permanent happiness which lead a person into a spiral of never-ending cravings and misery. On the other hand, restrained consumer habits or austerity and emphasis on internal development lead to blissful experiences of existence through transcendental knowledge and realization of the Ultimate Reality, which is the final destination of human life. The great sage and scholar Adi Sankara, thus, declares this truth in pith and substance:

श्लोकार्धेन प्रवक्ष्यामि यदुक्तं ग्रन्थकोटिभिः।
ब्रह्म सत्यं जगन्मिथ्या जीवो ब्रह्मैव नापरः॥

Adi Sankara had cast in a sentence what has been elaborated by scholars in millions of words in multiple books: *"ब्रह्मन्" (Brahman) is the only reality and the rest of the world has a relative or illusory existence; every creature on this planet manifests the Ultimate Reality".* This all-pervasive Ultimate Reality in our cosmic universe according to the great Acharya is nameless, formless and attribute-less. This does not mean non-existence of a visually-verifiable universe which is a gross form or manifestation of the Ultimate Reality called Brahman.

Physical scientists simply explain it to mean that matter is nothing but energy in another form. Excessively regulated by gross senses, understanding or creativity of individuals is based upon their gross perceptions. It, thus, follows that like the gross world, all creatures including those described as supernatural ones, Gods/ Goddesses, etc. too are manifestations of the nameless, formless and attribute-less energy or all-pervasive *Brahman*. It pervades the whole universe and is addressed by various names by sages and seers across the world.

Means and methods for realization of this Ultimate Reality have been described variously in ancient literatures of various religions depending upon the understanding, culture and preferences at the relevant point of time. Indeed, narratives of scriptures, including those in mythologies and religious rituals, are considered as means for creating a conducive environment for realization of Brahman. In other words, regular study of scriptures, religious rituals, pilgrimages, and constructive works done with a sense of detachment for the larger welfare of creatures becomes a conducive background for the realization of Brahman, the only truth. Adi Sankara, one of the greatest philosophers of all times, categorically declares that good actions done without indulgences and rituals are means for purification of Chitta, and not for realization of the only Ultimate Reality or Brahman. Realization of Brahman is impossible even by millions of good actions and religious rituals:

चित्तस्य शुद्धये कर्म न तु वस्तूपलब्धये।
वस्तुसिद्धिविचारेण न किंचित्कर्मकोटिभिः॥

In brief, the principle laid down unequivocally in the Vedanta philosophy is that even by good karmas performed without indulgences, repeated visits to temples, religious rituals, pilgrimages, etc., which are not coupled with uninterrupted deeper meditation (sadhana), can not lead to realization of Brahman or liberation of a human being from the bondage of this relative or illusory world. The cycle of life and death and worldly pleasures and pains will continue till the realization of Brahman. Adi Sankara illustrates this situation with the example of a person suffering from illness who fails to recover since he only recites the names of the medicines prescribed by the physician rather than punctually taking them. Like wise, experiencing Brahman is possible only through uninterrupted and focused sadhana. Mere recitation of the word Brahman and names of rituals does not lead to self-realization. Realization of Brahman is the same as self-realization. Atma or Self is the mirror image of Paramatma or Brahman, realization of which is the same as realization of Brahman:

न गच्छति विना पानं व्याधिरोषधशब्दतः।
विनापरोक्षानुभवैः ब्रह्मशब्दैर्न मुच्यते॥

It is clearly explained in Sanatan Dharma texts that working for the satisfaction of others without expectations and taking actions with detachment in the service of others is the real worship or service of God. Thus, it is exhorted that a wise person should always strive for happiness or satisfaction of others without caring for his comfort or pain:

येन केन प्रकारेण यस्य कस्यापि देहिनः।
सन्तोषं जनयेत्प्राज्ञः तदेवेश्वरपूजनम्।।

In the Sanatan tradition, dharma, artha, kama and moksha (धर्म, अर्थ, काम, मोक्ष) are known as the four pillars of human endeavour (पुरुषार्थ-चतुष्टय). This means that discharging duties in accordance with law and principles of morality, acquiring wealth through legitimate and moral means, leading a healthy sexual life without digression, and finally liberation from worldly bondage, are four equally important aspects of life. Ignoring one, or excessive emphasis on another, may cause imbalance in society which may potentially open windows for distortions or evasiveness, which is not good for its healthy growth. It is stated that a wise person should acquire knowledge and wealth assuming that he will never grow old, is indestructible and whose life has no end. But he should discharge his duties (धर्म) without losing a moment, actioning the requirements as if Death is holding him by the hair on his head, and he might not get another chance to lead his life in line with dharma:

अजरामरवत्प्राज्ञः विद्यामर्थं च चिन्तयेत्।
गृहीतमिव केशेषु मृत्युना धर्ममाचरेत्।।

Knowledge enlightens a human about right and wrong, and leads him towards emancipation from worldly bondage. As repeatedly underlined in the Upanishads- *"knowledge leads to immortality"* (*विद्ययाऽमृतमश्नुते*); *"knowledge is the one that results in emancipation"* (*सा विद्या या विमुक्तये*); *"there is no liberation without knowledge"* (*ऋते ज्ञानान्न मुक्तिः*); etc. Likewise, wealth earned through fair and moral means helps in leading a healthy life of sensual pleasure in a disciplined way and in performance of various actions in promoting dharma in addition to being an enabler for helping those in need and the society at large.

The great Sanskrit poet Kalidas in his epic book "*Raghuvansha Mahakavyam*" enumerates the attributes of the illustrious Raghu clan underlining that its members followed an ideal or a balanced life style represented by the four objects of human pursuits (पुरुषार्थ-चतुष्टय). Accordingly, its progeny spent the first part of life in receiving education, the second in earning wealth and thereby helping the needy and enjoying worldly pleasures, the third in leading the life of a detached ascetic, and finally demitting the body in the last part by applying a yogic practice:

शैशवेऽभ्यस्तविद्यानां यौवने विषयैषिणाम्।
वार्धक्ये मुनिवृत्तीनां योगेनान्ते तनुत्यजाम्।।

In other words, a disciplined and balanced life with equal emphasis on all the four objects of human pursuits (पुरुषार्थ-चतुष्टय)- dharma, artha, kama and moksha- was the secret of a contented life of hundred years. Sanatan Dharma proponents wished to lead such a healthy and satisfied life by praying- *"May we survive for hundred years to see, hear and remain healthy"* (*पश्येमशरदः शतम्, जीवेम शरदः शतम्, अदीनाः स्याम शरदः शतम्, भूयश्च शरदः शतात्*). The life of hundred years, divided into four parts -brahmacharya, grihastha, vanaprastha, and sanyasa – is intended to serve associated objectives depending upon the capability of people in respective age groups. Vanaprastha and sanyasa did not mean running away to the forest in saffron robes and forgetting social responsibilities. Some sages and seers have put it differently by saying that if a person fails to receive education in the first part of his life, does not acquire wealth in the second, or fails to lead a virtuous life in the third, he can hardly do anything worthwhile towards the end or in the last part of his life:

प्रथमे नार्जिता विद्या द्वितीये नार्जितं धनम्।
तृतीये नार्जितं पुण्यं चतुर्थे किं करिष्यति।।

Needless to repeat that the material world experienced through the senses, including gross eyes, which is described in terms of names and forms is also an expression of the same Ultimate Reality called Brahman.

It is to be recalled that Vedic or Sanatan civilization believes in harmonious survival of human beings with nature, both being manifestations of the same Reality. In sharp contrast, Western civilization is apparently unmindful of the implications of the destruction of nature on the essence of spirituality. Being composed in the peaceful environment of woods (अरण्य), a large chunk of Vedic texts is known as Aranyaka (आरण्यक). To meditate on the Ultimate Reality for self-realization, saints found ideal abode in the Himalayas or on the banks of rivers originating therefrom. Worldly distraction could not disturb them in the vibrant, pure and peaceful milieu of Himalayas. In Vedic literature, these places came to be known as the play-ground (क्रीड़ा-भूमि) of Gods and Goddesses and as meditation ground or tapo-bhoomi (तपोभूमि) of seers and sages (ऋषि-मुनि). These places stood purified due to the sylvan environment created by Gods-Goddesses and rishis-munis, and came to be popularly known as pilgrimages or tirthas.

Scholars and those engaged in creative pursuits too got attracted to these places. Slowly the attention of the whole world was drawn to them. It is, thus, no exaggeration to say that the tirthas preferred by sages and seers as their meditation ground or tapo-bhoomi, a location used contextually with deva-bhoomi (देव-भूमि) or play-ground of Gods and Goddesses, are known in ancient Indian literature as tirthas. The essence of holy Kailas and Manasarovar and how these became the Ultimate Tirtha, so close and yet so far, for such a large bulk of humanity cutting across many religions is taken up in later chapters.

According to the scriptures, the rich environment created by the sages and seers through their virtuous actions and meditation helps in purifying the thought processes of those undertaking pilgrimages to the tirthas and bring natural thinking to their mind. As a result, they are expected to become welfare-minded. The outcome of such visits is surely seen in terms of improved living conditions of the society through equitable sharing of resources essential for a healthy life. It is also found in terms of the creation of a conducive environment for those seeking liberation from bondage caused by their failure to differentiate between what is right from what is wrong. As the environs of tirthas remain spiritually charged, these help seekers find their respective path of meditation and other forms of spiritual endeavour. The natural environment of tirthas free from pollution, and the company of saints and evolved souls, altogether in a vibrant spiritual atmosphere, bring purity in the hearts and minds of seekers, which in turn makes their spiritual journey for experiencing the Absolute Truth or self-realization smoother. It may be appropriate to conclude that just by visiting the holy places and temples, one cannot reach the ultimate destination. Means can not be taken to be the end. Means are important milestones in the journey towards the ultimate goal, but to consider them to be the end amounts to promoting superstitions.

Patal Khand (पाताल खण्ड) of Padma Purana (पद्म पुराण) vividly describes the preparations for undertaking pilgrimage

(तीर्थ-यात्रा) in addition to underlining the essential qualifications for undertaking the venture. It has been laid down that after youth or in the later part of life, a human being needs to seek the shelter of the Almighty in order to swim across the worldly ocean. He should dedicate himself to the Omniscient, Omnipresent and Omnipotent, recite his names regularly, and remember him with offerings. Sacrificing his worldly cravings including sensual pleasures, he should place the Ultimate Reality in his heart and meditate. He should remain in awareness that the worldly pleasures are momentary and instead of bringing durable happiness to life, they lead to increased sufferings or outright misery of cravings. It is necessary for the seeker to internalize that absolute happiness lies in dedicating himself in devotion of God who is free from the cycle of birth, old age and death. For this, it is useful to avoid actions that hurt others and instead to enjoy the company of saints who are in a state of self-contentment having experienced the Ultimate Reality and thus are found enjoying blissful peace.

This can not happen without rejecting distractions caused by cravings, anger, greed, lust, attachment, etc. Blessings of saints who have already achieved the highest goal of self-realization greatly help in creating the ability to develop detachment from the world and achieve permanent peace of mind. Such saints are found in the spiritually-charged atmosphere of holy tirthas. Thus, men and women desirous to elevate themselves should undertake visits to such places to purify their hearts and minds by receiving the blessings of these great souls. This exercise is stated to help lead them to burn away their accumulated sins of past. It, thus, follows that every human being desirous to get rid of worldly fears or other bondages and anxious to swim across the worldly ocean should visit the holy tirthas.

They should do this carefully avoiding wrong actions and without causing any harm to the spiritually-charged atmosphere of such places, including their clean and pure water and natural surroundings to be eligible to get the blessings of sages and seers residing there:

वलीपलितदेहो वा यौवनेनान्वितोऽपि वा।
ज्ञात्वा मृत्युमनिस्तीर्य हरिं शरणमाब्रजेत्।।

तत्कीर्तने तत्श्रवणे वन्दने तस्य पूजने।
मतिरेव प्रकर्तव्या नान्यत्र वनितादिषु।।

सर्वं नश्वरमालोक्य क्षणस्थायि सुदुःखदम्।
जन्ममृत्युजरातीतं भक्तिवल्लभमच्युतम्।।

स हरिर्ज्ञायते साधू संगमात्पापवर्जितात्।।
येषां कृपातः पुरुषा भवन्त्यसुखवर्जिताः।।

ते साधवः शान्तिरागाः कामक्रोधविवर्जिताः।
ब्रुवन्ति यन्महाराज तत्संसारनिवर्तकम्।।

तीर्थेषु लभ्यते साधू रामचन्द्रपरायणः।
यद्दर्शनं नृणां पापराशिदाहाषु सुक्षणि।।

तस्मात्तीर्थेषु गन्तव्यं नरैः संसारभीरुभिः।
पुण्योदकेषु सततं साधुश्रेणिविराजिषु।।

In Narada Purana (नारद पुराण), those showing enthusiasm and interest in pilgrimage have been cautioned and told about the required qualities for undertaking such ventures. The importance of pilgrimage has also been elaborated in this mythological text. It has been said that the real benefits of a tirtha-yatra can be derived by only those who are in control of their senses in thought, words and action; are completely filled with a sense of self-satisfaction and a passion for helping others; and remain untouched by arrogance in any form. A person wishing to undertake a tirtha-yatra has been urged to remember that elements that work as impediments in achieving the desired results, such as, craving, anger, greed, lust, arrogance, etc. have to be shunned completely. The tirtha-yatri's heart should be as pure as gold and in no case should he deviate from the virtuous path. It is incumbent upon him to be spontaneous in showing fellow-feelings towards every creature and respect others in the same way as he likes his self-respect. Reverence, sedateness of mind, patience and self-control are indispensable attributes of a pilgrim or tirtha-yatri. People without these attributes - sinners, atheists, self-centred and those of doubtful nature - remain deprived of the expected benefits even after undertaking repeated tirthayatras to holy places. Visits taken with a purified heart, extricates from the sins committed in this life, but pilgrimage undertaken with an impure heart fails to deliver the desired fruits. It is added that the sins committed in holy places or in tirthas cannot be remedied. It, therefore, follows that people in control of desire, anger, greed, lust, arrogance, attachment, etc. undertaking visits to tirthas only derive the expected affects of such visits. In that case, those seeking access to heaven or absolute bliss succeed in achieving their cherished goals. The following observations made in Narada Purana are worth pondering over:

गंगादि तीर्थेषु वसन्ति मत्स्याः देवालये पक्षिगणाश्चरन्ति।।
भावोज्झितास्ते न फलं लभन्ते तीर्थाच्च देवायतनाच्च मुख्यात्।।

भावं ततो हृत्कमले निधाय तीर्थानि सेवेत समाहितात्मा।।

The sense conveyed through these verses of Narada Purana is that even though fish reside in tirthas of the river Ganga, etc. and birds are seen roaming inside temples where Gods are known to reside, but these creatures do not receive the actual benefits for living in tirtha and temples as they are devoid of heartfelt divinity. Thus, pilgrims with divinity in their hearts and self-control should enjoy visits to holy places.

It becomes clear from a careful study of Vedic literature and other scriptures that the history of pilgrimage to holy places is as old as human culture and civilization itself. Communication facilities and residential infrastructure as we find today hardly existed in the distant past. But, people with an inquisitive mind in the quest of peace and permanent bliss did not care for the risks and difficulties on account of lack of personal comforts, inadequate road infrastructure, lack of medical facilities, unknown terrain, and adverse weather conditions in negotiating the distances on foot to reach the holy places situated far and wide in the most-difficult and secluded regions. Even in modern times, resource-rich people with limited faith or interest in spirituality are found eager to undertake the arduous journeys to remotely-located holy places and shrines to derive peace and happiness like those visiting these places with conviction in scriptures and spiritual commitments. It is not to say that a guiding spirit of curiosity or a sense of adventure to visit the tirthas is fraught with sin or wrong; as long as respect for spirituality sought by others and of the holy place itself is judiciously and meticulously maintained, it may amount to nothing more than a missed opportunity to achieve the Ultimate Reality.

Under the influence of increasing degrees of consumerism and a distinct bias towards materialism, it is being noticed that the importance of religious shrines and tirthas is enhancing more for commercial considerations than religious or spiritual factors. Fast-paced developments in communication infrastructure, including transportation and telecom, and in hospitality facilities in and around the tirthas have turned many of these places into commercial hubs. Without doubt they have become sources of livelihood and enrichment for many who serve the visitors. Religious tourism is the new fad. Resultantly, the natural environment of these places is deteriorating due to pollution in various forms, which disturbs the true pilgrims. It is paradoxical that while ancient Indian tradition underlined the need for earning wealth for implementing the tenets of dharma, what we find today is prevalence of unnecessary distortions in the guise of religious rituals being held at tirthas for acquiring and accumulating more wealth! In the process, superstitions and bigotry start receiving respectability, which incidentally had no place in Sanatan Dharma. Certainly, this issue deserves serious introspection.

It is explained briefly that tirthas remained charged or spiritually vibrant as they treasured undiluted and unlimited natural beauty coupled with austere life-styles and self-elevating explorations of sages and seers, who avoided worldly indulgences and materialism to remain engaged on the path of self-realization. This has been stated expressly by the author of Shuddha Tatva (शुद्ध तत्त्व)–

प्रभावादद्भुताद् भूमेः सलिलस्य च तेजसः।
परिग्रहात् मुनीनां च तीर्थानां पुण्यता स्मृता।।

(The purity of tirthas is attributable to the influence of land, water and natural energy besides surroundings of sages and seers.)

This is the reason why travellers on the path of spirituality have been visiting remotely-located holy places regardless of extreme hardships. They were attracted and charged up by their energizing, spiritually-vibrant and elevating environment. That is how spiritually-inclined inquisitive seekers and explorers never got exhausted in taking rounds of Himalayan peaks, valleys and origins of rivers considered as homes of various deities and hermits. Since aeons, some of the holiest of the holy shrines remain situated in those geographically most-difficult locations. Sages and seers did not like to leave these places as the loss of absolute bliss they experienced in solitude could not be compensated by creature comforts and material goods elsewhere. Some of the most insightful spiritual literature and mythological texts were composed in these holy places.

It is ironical that the so-called civilized and busy gentry of the present age seen indulging in materialism driven by conspicuous consumption seems to want to have an experience of spiritual bliss by visiting those tirthas that have maximum aids in terms of hospitality industry and physical infrastructure and which can be thus reached in the shortest possible time. Very few sages and seers could succeed in experiencing this bliss and that too only after arduous meditative practices over ages and many-many lives. Lord Krishna said it aptly in the Gita–

> बहूनां जन्मनामन्ते ज्ञानवान्मां प्रपद्यते।
>
> *(The knower succeeds in experiencing this bliss in my proximity after efforts lasting over many births.)*
>
> अनेकजन्मसंसिद्धः ततो याति परां गतिम्
>
> *(Only after treading on the arduous spiritual path with karmas performed continuously without expectations over many births, a seeker could reach that stage to experience absolute bliss.)*

For those wanting the best of both worlds, such yester-year sermons hardly convey any meaning regardless of its increasing relevance.

India was always a socio-cultural unit with its geographical limits stretching from the greater Himalayas to the Indian ocean. Study of ancient scriptures, including the mythological texts, substantiates that Kailas-Manasarovar are amongst the holiest of holy places on this planet for the followers of Sanatan Dharma across the greater Indian sub-continent. Dwellers here, regardless of their religious affiliations or even those devoid of spiritual inclinations, were deeply influenced by the mesmerising natural beauty of Kailas-Manasarovar. Believers in Sanatan Dharma perceived them as the most beautiful part of heaven – a play field for Gods and Goddesses and abode of ancient sages and seers.

It is but natural that experiences of a seeker visiting holy places would differ from those of other inquisitive explorers. The great saint and explorer of repute Swami Pranavanand in his book "*Kailas-Manasarovar*", published in 1949 underlines this difference beautifully–

> *"In the surroundings of the holy Kailas and Manasarovar, even the most wandering mind, to whichever religion it may belong – whether to Hinduism or Buddhism, Christianity or Islam, whether to atheism or agnosticism– becomes concentrated and irresistibly, unknowingly or unconsciously drawn as if propelled by someone from behind to the Divine Presence that is hidden behind this apparently vast universe; while a good Sadhak may enter into sublime ecstasies involuntarily. But just as a man, the mucus membrane of whose nose has become dull, can not perceive the sweet odour of a rose, and just as a radio set cannot receive a song from a foreign programme unless it is set to a proper wavelength of that place, even so it is no wonder that a person devoid of any spiritual tendencies can not perceive or feel the effect of the spiritual vibrations existing in a particular place".*

Whatever may be the objective, pilgrims need to remain sensitive towards the natural, spiritual and cultural environment of tirthas. Even if they remain short of experiencing the spiritual energy or vibrations of these places, the pollution-free natural atmosphere does educate and benefit them. By maintaining their sanctity, there would also be no adverse impact on local cultures in and around such places and shrines. Even the so-called religion-centric tourism will fail to sustain by compromising the integrity of tirthas. In the scriptures, nature has been described as a munificent mother offering everything to her children without any expectation. This character of nature deserves to be preserved and respected to remember her 'giving' quality and sacrifices. Pilgrims to eco-sensitive holy places should internalize that it was completely atrocious and outrageous behaviour against Draupadi, the most compelling character of the great epic *Mahabharata* that caused the most devastating destruction in the war that ensued. Increasing number of calamities and human casualties that are taking place in the eco-sensitive zones of Himalayas need to be viewed as largely attributable to human atrocities in various forms including irresponsible conduct of some tourists, explorers and so-called pilgrims. Greater sensitivity, thus, needs to be shown to avoid disasters before it is too late.

Kailas-Manasarovar yatra has become easier with the passage of time. Paved roads now reach up to Lipulekh Pass, and within Tibet right up to the base/shores of Kailas-Manasarovar. Only the parikramas need be done on foot. Guest houses, tea-shops, and access to nearby habitats en-route have also been progressively developed within India, and even more so in Tibet. Holy persons, pilgrims, explorers and tourists are becoming more inquisitive about the cultural and religious aspects of holy places; at the same time, paradoxically, these places are being increasingly used for commercialisation and exhibitive tendencies.

Sadly, spirituality seems to be taking a back seat. Religious practices are underscored by commercial ventures amounting to outright fraud in some cases. We need not only to be aware of this disturbing trend, but also be careful not to cross the limits. Moreover, if pilgrims or religious tourists are unable to contribute to improving the environment, they should at least avoid deteriorating it. One could see large quantities of plastic waste for which some pilgrims and religious tourists are singularly responsible not only en-route to Kailas-Manasarovar but also in the habitats at the base of holy Kailas and all along its parikrama. The shores of Manasarovar and proximate waters show signs of human neglect and negligence. Wasted food-stuff, its packaging, and non-degradable materials used in religious rituals lying scattered around are unlikely to pacify the so-called spiritual quest of pilgrims. There is also no possibility of any other intended benefits coming on their way, besides causing grief to fellow yatris who have a more disciplined intent. Indeed, nothing could be more sinful if actions of pilgrims lead to environmental deterioration. Scriptures are found exhorting that sins committed elsewhere get washed by penance performed in holy places, but sins committed in tirthas leave permanent scars; they remain unremedied–

अन्यक्षेत्रे कृतं पापं तीर्थक्षेत्रे विनश्यति।
तीर्थक्षेत्रे कृतं पापं वज्रलेपो भविष्यति

2

Kailas-Manasarovar in Himalayas stands Highest among Sacred Mountains

Curiosity, and explorations to satisfy it, have defined human nature. These have been shaping our socio-cultural ethos and civilization in varied forms and manifestations. The tall peaks of craggy young mountains, origins of mighty untamed rivers, deep silent valleys and gorges, twists and turns of waterfalls, and tranquil large water bodies in the high reaches of mountains have all been viewed by the evolving human society as divinity personified in material form. This is common to most societies and cultures the world over. Purity or holiness has been associated with many mountains, rivers and lakes. Their majestic isolation has held a mysterious and mystic lure for the inquisitive and bold. Dense forests with fast-changing flora and fauna as you climb up the mountain ranges not only present nature in its purest form, but are associated with innumerable traditions and lore which paint them as abode of the Creator of the Universe and of local deities. Probably this is one reason why these places have retained their pristine glory to a large extent despite the onslaught by excessively materialistic endeavours of the human race as time passes.

Purity and holiness of mountains world-wide

Many religious customs, cultural traditions and myths are also linked with tall mountain ranges in different parts of the world. Mountain peaks considered to be the abode of Gods-Goddesses, sages and seers have remained vibrant and alive in the consciousness of mankind. They continue to attract the attention of the explorer and spiritually-inclined inquisitive mind, alike. Ancient texts and traditions call for maintaining the purity of life-sustaining mountains, rivers, lakes and forests.

Study of ancient literature, including unwritten lore and traditions, reveals a universality in relation to the religious and spiritual importance attached to many mountains or mountain ranges. Sanctification of a mountain in fact lies in the legends and myths associated with sages and mystics who lived in the deep mountain wilderness. Mount Fuji is viewed as holy by traditional Japanese society, considering it to be the abode of Fire God.

A notable narrative of the Bible, containing the most celebrated religious text of Christianity, asserts that, like Mount Zion, people having faith in God can not be shaken. Mount Olympus for the ancient Greeks, and Mount Sinai in Egypt, are both viewed as mountain homes of the Gods. According to the religious tradition of Jews, Mount Sinai (at 2,285 metres) is believed to be a holy mountain and the construction of the temple at its base was done as per the direction of God. It is held that Prophet Moses, who is also described in Hebrew Bible as Prince of ancient Egypt, alone could trek to this holy mountain. Also, many Christians believe that this is the mountain where God spoke to Moses and gave him the Ten Commandments, and this belief has drawn pilgrims to its summit for over 2,000 years. Local lore of more than one faith is seen attached to one mountain.

In Europe, the French-Italian Alps include Mont Blanc (4,810 metres) also known as white mountain. Mount Rocciamelone (3,538 metres) in Italy, near the French border, is also associated with a number of Christian traditional beliefs– one such tradition involves trekking up Mount Rocciamelone with the statue of the Virgin Mary. It is also said that a three-metre tall statue of Virgin Mary was installed on its peak in the year 1899.

Believers of Islam in the Middle East do not recognise idols nor believe in worshiping symbols. But those inhabiting the Kyrgyz area are seen bending in respectful devotion for a glance of Mount Mumtaz Ada. They are convinced that this mount was inhabited by 70 ascetic Muslim monks or fakirs, which included Musa and Ali.

Adam Peak is a famous mountain of Sri-Lanka at 2,243 metres. Also called 'Sri Pad' or 'Mountain of Shiva's Light', the sacred foot-print on a 1.8 metre rock formation at its summit is believed variously to be that of Lord Buddha by Buddhists, of Shiva or Hanuman in Hindu tradition, of Saint Thomas by Christians, and of Prophet Mohammad by followers of Islam. Regardless of their religious affiliations, people uniformly believe in the sanctity of this mountain.

Mount Kinabalu (4,095 metres), a sacred mountain in Malaysia, is a most recognisable symbol of Sabah. It has been a sacred resting ground of the dead. The indigenous Kadazan-Dusun tribe are buried facing the mountain in the belief that their spirit would reach Kinabalu without difficulty. As per local lore, the spirits remain inside this 'graveyard' until they pass into afterlife known as Libabou.

Mount Agung or Gunung Agung, is an active sacred volcano located on the island of Bali in the Indonesia island arc at an elevation of 3,031 metres. The Balinese believe that it is the abode of the Gods. It is on this volcano that the famous temple Pura Besakih is located, which can be reached after climbing hundreds of steps.

In ancient Chinese cultural literature, value and purity of mountains have been explained repeatedly. It is revealing to note that the Chinese phrase for pilgrimage ("*ch'ao-shan chin-hsiang*") means 'paying one's respect to a mountain'. Mount Tai Shan, venerated by them as their most sacred mountain since the third millennium BC, was not merely the mountain home of the Gods, but was regarded as a deity itself. This son of Emperor of Heaven mediated between humans and God, and 7,000 stairs were stated to have been constructed for trekking up Mount Tai Shan.

Within China, the famous philosopher Laozi ("Old Master"), who lived in the fifth or sixth century BC and said to be a senior contemporary of Confucius, taught his disciples to have extraordinary and respectful devotion for mountains as they are imbued with sacred energy. Taoism is considered to be both a philosophical tradition and an organized religion. Its followers, the Taoist/ Daoist, make pilgrimage to 5 sacred mountains in eastern China, besides some others in order to pray at the temples and absorb spiritual energy from these holy places. These sacred places are believed to be governed by immortals.

In the first century AD, merchants returning from India via the Silk Route began the introduction of Buddhism into China. As Buddhism spread its wings into China, like Taoist hermits the Buddhists monks too favoured the high mountains and dense forests for their meditative practices. Initially they set up small hermitages, which were expanded into large monastic complexes at many peaks (some of which were previously held sacred by Taoists). Over time, 4 peaks considered to be the dwelling place of a Bodhisattva emerged as having primary sanctity among the Buddhists–

- Wu Tai Shan (3,061 metres; Shanxi) sacred to Manjushri, Bodhisattva of Wisdom;
- Pu Tuo Shan (284 metres; Zhejiang) sacred to Avalokitesvara, Bodhisattva of Compassion;
- Emei Shan (3,099 metres; Sichuan) sacred to Samantabhadra, Bodhisattva of Benevolent Action; and
- Jiu Hua Shan (1,341 metres; Anhui) sacred to Kshitigarbha, Bodhisattva of Salvation.

The teachings of Confucius, a unique promoter of cultured and courteous behavioural exchange in society, are based on his realization that like river water, human mind is a flow of thoughts which requires stability of a mountain to make a man benevolent. Confucius described mountains as symbols of greatness and benevolence–

> "*The wise take pleasure in water, but the benevolent in mountain, because wisdom moves about but benevolence remains still, wisdom leads to happiness, benevolence to long life*".

Mythological tales related to Africa narrate that the highest peak of Mount Kenya is the abode of the local deity Ngai (Muen Nyaga). Mount Kilimanjaro (the White Mountain), Africa's highest mountain, is considered sacred by the Chaga tribe, Tanzania's third largest ethnic group. The only active 'sodium carbonate' volcano in the world is in Tanzania. Called Ol Doinyo Lengai (the Mountain of God), it is believed by the pastoral Maasai tribe to be the home of their God Engai. With its strangely thin, silvery lava, it is a place of pilgrimage for them, who travel there to entreat their god Engai for rain, cattle, and children. Hardly surprising that this sacred mountain is less than 70 miles from the famed Olduval Gorge, a treasure-trove of 3.6 million-year-old hominin footprints at a site called Laetoli, and a "dance hall" of around 400 ancient homo sapiens' footprints (5,000 to 19,000 years' old) in the mudflats embossed in the lava of this mountain at a site called Engare Sero.

In New Zealand, the life of Taranaki aboriginals' centres around Mount Taranaki (2,518metres), which is extremely sacred to them. The tribe – living near to the mountain – also relies on rivers that flowed down from it to feed their plants, animals and to provide their living. As such, it has been a vital part of their heritage.

Indigenous Yakutat people inhabiting around Mount Saint Elias, the fourth tallest in North America at 5,489 metres, believe that their deity resided in this mountain peak, blessing them continuously by raising his head.

Many myths surround Mount Shasta in Northern California. Indigenous Modok people believe that God made an ice mountain on Shasta at creation. Then he drilled a big hole in heaven to bring down Planet Earth from there. When the ice mountain became green with curious creatures, God came down from heaven to make this mountain his abode. Other native Americans feel that the mountain was the sacred centre of the universe, being the home of the creator. It is especially important to the Wintu tribe, who trace their people's origin back to a sacred spring on the mountain.

For the Mayan Civilisation of Central America, "nature" essentially meant mountains, and amounted to the entire world, the work of God, everything marvellous and everything dangerous. Ethno-archaeological explorations of several Mayan sacred sites reveal that mountain-tops and mountain-top shrines are some of the most potent places in contemporary Maya highlands. Much of ancient Maya art and architecture expresses cosmology through the concept and images of a "Flower Mountain", the "axis mundi" or the dwelling place of Gods that rises out of a watery underworld and connects it to the sky. It serves as the connection between the Gods and Earth, and communication happens through caves, flowery mouths of the mountain and Gods.

Extensive references in ancient lore and literature reveal that for South American countries too mountains are traditionally associated with holiness and are considered homes of God or local deities. The Aztec Civilization linked with Mexico believed that for good crop production, it was necessary to worship mountains. Animals used to be sacrificed on mountain peaks to propitiate local deities said to be residing there for good rains and good harvests. Coatepec or Serpent Mountain was a most sacred place of Aztec mythology and religion, believed to be the site of the birth of Aztec/Mexica patron deity Huitzilopochtli.

The Andes Mountain ranges, extending over 2,000 miles in South America, have multiple peaks described in their local traditions as holy abodes of various Gods. According to the Inca mythology, there are three realms: Hanan Pacha (upper realm), Kay Pacha (human realm), and Uku Pacha (inner world, or underworld). Mountains—rising up from the human world toward Hanan Pacha—offered the Incas a connection with their most powerful gods in the heavens. Apas is reportedly the most powerful God among them and resides in the sacred peak called Mount Ausangate (6,384 metres) in Peru. The local tradition believes that Apas is a representative of the Sun and it is necessary to offer sacrifices to please him.

The Incas carried out some of the most dramatic rituals and ceremonies known to mankind from ancient times on sacred features of natural landscape. Archaeological excavations show that groups of people walked hundreds of miles across mountainous terrain on pilgrimages involving human sacrifices (capacochas) on very high mountain summits. Mount Llullaillaco (6,739 metres) has the world's highest such archaeological site.

Hindu holy mountains and rivers

Sacred places are a prominent feature in India. In most cases, the sacredness of a place is linked in some way or the other to natural objects such as trees, groves, gardens, water bodies, caves, landscapes and mountains. These sacred forms and shapes that are derived from natural objects and features often become symbolic or emblematic. Throughout India, mountains are revered as mysterious places with the power to evoke an overwhelming sense of the sacred. For people of many different sub-cultures within India, that mystery and sense of the sacred imbues their existence with meaning and vitality.

While mountains may be considered sacred in various ways, certain peaks are designated as sacred by particular religious traditions and are enveloped with myths, beliefs and religious practices. For example, Mount Kailas (in Tibet) is regarded as the abode of Lord Shiva.

Among the mountains in India intimately linked with Mount Kailas are the remaining four of *Panch-Kailas*. Of these, Adi-Kailas (6,191 metres) is in Uttarakhand. Like Mount Kailas, Adi Kailas is also replete with a Parvati Sarovar and Gauri Kund. There is a shrine near Parvati Sarovar, which is sometimes visited by swan-like birds. Kinnaur-Kailas which is reached through Charang La pass, Shrikhand Kailas or Shrikhand Mahadev in the Great Himalayan National Park, and Manimahesh or Chamba Kailas, all three in Himachal Pradesh.

A mountain may also be associated with the activities of holy persons or beings or may contain sacred sites such as temples and groves. For example, Mount Govardhan at

Vrindavan is revered for its association with Lord Krishna. This Parvat, which was raised by Lord Krishna to protect the inhabitants of Vrindavan from the wrath of Indra, the God of Rain, was the child-God's play ground.

Certain mountains that may not be considered sacred in any traditional sense are revered as places of spiritual attainment. For example, Arunachala Mountain at Tiruvannamalai is revered by people and saints as a place for spiritual attainment. Throughout the world people look up to mountains as sources of blessings such as water, life, fertility and healing. Thus, hundreds of millions revere the Himalayas, the A bode of Snow, as the source of sacred rivers, such as the Ganga, on whose life-giving waters they depend for their very existence.

In India, mountains have special significance within Sanatan culture. Vindhya Mountains, which separate the North from Deccan Plateau, are cited repeatedly in the Epics and Puranas. Millions also visit the pilgrimage sites in various mountains from north to south and east of west such as Agastya-mala in Kerala, Shathashrunga Parvat (100-peaked mountain) and Malayagiri both in Karnataka, Tirumala hills in Andhra Pradesh, Sahyadri hills in Maharashtra, Girinar in Gujarat, Amarkantak in Madhya Pradesh, and Kamaksha hills in Assam, all of which are considered spiritually-vibrant holy cultural centres.

By far the maximum concentration of sacred mountains anywhere in the world is to be found in the towering Himalayas and dense forests in its lower reaches. The region has been considered an ideal place for seekers, providing a serene, peaceful and conducive atmosphere to pursue the most arduous path of meditation and spirituality without any distraction. Mount Kanchenjunga, the third highest peak in the world at 8,586 metres, literally means "the five treasures of snow" or "five repositories of God", namely, gold, silver, gems, grain and the holy scriptures.

The majestic peaks and valleys of Himalayas have been recognized as the 'play field' and receptacle of Gods and Goddesses. Spiritual explorations pursued by sages, seers and mystics of the Himalayas led them to the realization of the Ultimate Reality leading to their experience-based conclusion that there is no real difference between a living being (Soul or जीवात्मा) and God (Prime Soul or परमात्मा). Our creation in terms of reality is based upon perception attributable to limited understanding.

Through sustained search and explorations within, and without support of external scientific tools for validation, the sages and seers of the Himalayas confidently declared that the whole universe was nothing but a manifestation of the nameless, formless and attributeless Ultimate Reality in gross form and what is ascertained through gross senses is based on illusion or relativity. They propounded coexistence of humanity in harmony with nature, and through it underlined that to be in service of other living beings, who are like themselves mirror images of the Creator, is the real service of God. For them the entire world was one family or like a nest of birds (वसुधैव कुटुम्बकम्, विश्वं भवत्येकनीड़म्). Unity in diversity was the slogan of saints evolving themselves in the lap of the Himalayas without rejecting the relative reality of the material world. Vedic civilization and a huge body of spiritual literature including scriptures and mythological texts were created in the creative environment of Himalayas and on the banks of rivers originating from these mountains. Universal substantive thoughts in these books still remain valid and have withstood the scrutiny of time.

As set out in brief earlier, nature in various forms and manifestations is described as the gross expression of the

Ultimate Reality, called by different denominations, such as, *Brahman*, *Parameshwar*, *Paramatma*, *Paramatattva*, etc. Rivers originating from holy mountains, particularly from the Himalayan ranges, are also known as tirthas. Bathing, meditative practices, penance, etc. performed on the banks of these rivers are considered conducive for the pursuit of self-realization, getting rid of accumulated sins, for access to heaven or for material prosperity depending upon the choices to be exercised.

In addition to scriptures, poetic expressions of creative writers contain extensive descriptions of the natural beauty of the Himalayas. The Sanskrit poet Kalidas who is known as the Guru of all poets starts his great epic *Kumarsambhavam* highlighting the physical beauty, cosmology, ecology and other attributes of the Himalayas. He describes the Himalayas as the soul of divinity and king of all mountains. Situated in the northerly direction, deep into the oceans on the east and west, the Himalayas, according to the poet, stand on the Earth as if they are its principal pole or measuring rod. He refers to a mythological tale according to which Mother Earth finding herself excessively exploited and in pain, took the form of a cow and hid herself. This led to loud lamentations by the subjects of the God-incarnate King Prithu, as they had no water to drink and no food to eat. This angered the King, who armed with his bow and arrows, went out in search of Mother Earth. Fearing her destruction, Mother Earth in the form of a cow, appeared before the King and agreed to be milked. Having been milked by many, when Mount Kailas took the form of a milkman, precious shining stones and medicines were extracted from the Mother Earth. The role of calf was played by the Himalayas at that stage. The precious shining stones, medicines, etc. received in abundance were used by the great King Prithu (in whose name the Earth is called Prithvi) to serve his subjects. Geological conditions found in the snow-capped Himalayas help produce many varieties and large quantities of precious stones, do not affect its unique beauty in any way:

अस्त्युत्तरस्यां दिशि देवतात्मा हिमालयो नाम नगाधिराजः।
पूर्वापरौ तोयनिधीवगाह्य स्थितः पृथिव्यामिव मानदण्डः।।

यं सर्वशैलाः परिकल्प्य वत्सं मेरौ स्थिते दोग्धरि दोहदक्षे।
भास्वन्ति रत्नानि महौषधिश्च पृथूपदिष्टां दुदुहुर्धरित्रीम्।।
अनन्तरत्नप्रभवस्य यस्य हिमं न सौभाग्यविलोपि जातम्।।

It is abundantly evident from the Rigveda, the oldest book known to man, that Vedic sages and seers were deeply influenced not only by the undiluted beauty of the Himalayas, but were also aware of the different floras and faunas found there, including their medicinal value. Purusha Sukta (पुरुष सूक्त) in the tenth chapter (दशम मण्डल) of this Vedic text contains the wishes of the composer Rishi- "*May these snow-clad mountains and gardens bestow happiness on us*" (यस्य मे हिमवन्तो...). The first epic written by Sage Valmiki, the *Ramayana*, and the greatest epic, the *Mahabharata*, written by Sage Vyasa are full of references of the soaring heights, steep-sided jagged peaks of Himalayan mountains, alpine glaciers, deeply-cut valleys, unfathomable river gorges and lakes, complex geologic structures, and vast meadows with their rich biodiversity and nibble-footed big cats and other fauna. There are clear and multiple references to Kailas and Manasarovar. The sage-poets Valmiki and Vyasa have expounded at length to draw out the austere lives of rishis and munis enjoying their blissful existence in the company of Himalayan deities and other supernatural inhabitants. Lord Krishna in the *Gita* eulogizes the Himalayas saying that he stands in the form of the Himalayas among the immovable or inanimate objects (स्थावराणां हिमालयः). He again identifies himself with Mount Kailas among all mountain peaks (मेरु: शिखरिणामहम्).

In mythological texts and sub-texts, purity and holiness of Himalayas, which include Kailas-Manasarovar and a number of rivers with their origins in Himalayan ranges, have been narrated in detail. Lord Shiva who is also known as Neelkanth (नीलकण्ठ) for voluntarily swallowing and retaining the poison, produced after the ocean was churned, in his throat, preferred Mount Kailas as the most suitable place to neutralize the destructive effects of the poison absorbed by him to save others. He found Mount Kailas as an ideal place for his meditation and solitude. It hardly requires mention that when the Gods were robbed of their powers and were displaced from heaven by the demons, they went to the Himalayas to propitiate Goddess Parvati, and answering their prayers, she appeared before them. Finally, the demons were slayed, and power and kingdom were restored to the Gods in Heaven.

Ganga, the river of Gods enjoyed privileges in her position at the feet of Lord Vishnu in Heaven. As the mythology informs, pleased with the prayers of King Bhagirath, it is Lord Vishnu who desired the selfless holy river's landfall high in the Himalayas for liberating King Bhagirath's forefathers caught up in the web of their sins. For this, only Lord Shiva meditating at Mount Kailas had the required strength to bear the full force of her landing on Earth all the way from Heaven by capturing her in his hair. Lord Shiva had to keep her engaged, wandering in the tresses of his long-matted hair for some time to dispel her pride and haughtiness, before allowing her to spring out and fall on Earth's surface. Besides emancipating the forefathers of sage King Bhagirath, the holy river obliged other seekers by liberating them from worldly shackles. Thus, after flowing from the head of

Lord Shiva, Ganga traverses the land from Himalayas to Ganga Sagar.

It may be necessary to demystify here the question as to how the origin of this holy river on Earth could be Gomukh/ Gangotri. Surely, it had to be where Lord Shiva, the only one capable of controlling the force of the mighty Ganga, was seated in deep meditation in solitude on Mount Kailas? A faithful study of mythological texts leaves no scope for any such question. Indeed, the abode of Lord Shiva is not confined to Mount Kailas despite numerous tales depicting this peak as his favourable sojourn. Lord Shiva rests in the Himalayas in the commonly-used refrain in mythological texts (हरः शेते हिमालये). Moreover, most rivers originating in the Himalayas carry the suffix Ganga, such as Bhagirathi Ganga, Ban Ganga, Mandakini Ganga, Alaknanda Ganga, Kali Ganga, Gori Ganga, Dhauli Ganga, Sarayu Ganga, Ram Ganga, etc. The word Ganga in generic and poetic sense is suggestive of purity or holiness.

It needs to be recalled that the stream originating from holy Kailas is known as "*Lha Chhu*" (in Tibetan language), which means "water of God". "*Sur Nadi*" and "*Sur Sarita*" are her other names in our ancient texts. The six-mile long natural canal that channelizes the surplus water of Lake Manasarovar to the adjoining lake, Rakshastal or "Ravan Hrada", is also called "*Ganga Chhu*", which means Ganga river or Ganga water. It may not be appropriate to confine Lord Shiva geospatially to a limited territory of the Himalayas. After all, he is the one who consumed the most dangerous poison to protect others, and whose name means an auspicious God, besides being the one who can be pleased easily and is concerned about the well-being of the whole world. How can He be confined to a limited land mass? The scholarly traditions of ancient Indian literature and oral traditional wisdom tell us to derive the real meaning of mythological, symbolic or hyperbolic expressions without losing sense of the substantive message.

It may be mentioned that river Karnali originating from Kailas-Manasarovar region which reaches Bahraich district of Uttar Pradesh via Nepal is known locally as Ghagra. When it passes through Ayodhya, the river is called Sarayu. Finally, it forms part of river Ganga in Chhapra district of Bihar. In Valmiki's *Ramayana*, Manasarovar is described as the origin of Sarayu. Thus, instead of getting confused by superficial reading of ancient texts, it may be useful to understand the real connotations of expressions seemingly appearing incoherent or paradoxical. If we analyse the geography correctly, it can be seen that the aerial distance from the origin of Alaknanda, Mandakini and Bhagirathi rivers is not much from Kailas-Manasarovar region. Before the annexation of Tibet by China, saints and pilgrims had been undertaking multiple journeys of Kailas-Manasarovar through places which are origins of holy rivers on the Indian side of the Himalayas. In ancient Indian texts, many access points or mountain passes have been mentioned for pilgrimage of Kailas-Manasarovar which include entry through Gangotri, Badrinath, Kedarnath, etc.

The famous Swedish explorer, geographer, topographer, photographer and travel writer, Dr. Sven Anders Hedin, after visiting and seeing Kailas-Manasarovar published his great work in the form of a book in 1909 "*Trans Himalayas*". Deeply impressed by the divine beauty and spiritual aura of Kailas-Manasarovar, he gave expression to his feelings, and observed that followers of other religions and foreigners generally do not like to convey respectful devotion to the mountains and rocks made of stones and soil. But after seeing Mount Kailas, they get filled with awe and devotion as this kind of holy mountain does not exist anywhere else in this world.

Similar expression has been given to his experiences by Edwin Bernbaun in his famous book, "*Sacred Mountains of the World*":

> "*Kailas has an extraordinary setting and appearance. Kailas looks more like a piece of marble sculpture fashioned by the hands of God, than a mountain created by forces of nature*".

In Hindu pantheon, Mount Kailas is Lord Shiva in another form. Adorned with long, matted, snowy hair, Lord Shiva himself is seen in a meditating posture in the shape of Mount Kailas. In ancient religious texts of Jainism and Buddhism too, the holiness of Kailas and Manasarovar has been mentioned extensively. Followers of Jainism hold that their first *Tirthankara* achieved emancipation at Kailas. Tibetan Buddhist tradition believes that Kailas is the Centre or Navel of the Universe. Its peak is a pagoda and Kailas is the shining abode of the great Damchok Buddha.

Sacred mountains nurture and protect, if conserved

Mountains are comprehensive ecosystems. Due to their topographic and bio-cultural richness they provide opportunities for climate change adaptation and act as a refuge for plants and animals both from environmental change and from competing species. They often play a vital role in a species' survival by providing opportunities for the species to move up and down and adapt to climate change. Sacred mountains have thus played an important role in conservation of local ecology and environment. In fact, a variety of themes are often found within sacred mountain traditions. It has been observed by environmental scientists that the beliefs embody a vital link between a community's cultural identity and traditional patterns of land conservation.

A finely-balanced relationship often was seen to be extolled in ancient literature between communities and their holy mountain in maintaining and preserving their natural resources in pristine conditions. Indigenous communities have long realized the value of high diversity and natural resources within mountains. Furthermore, mountains are resources of nature which nurture. The sacred mountain protected as a result of cultural beliefs, results in precious water, timber, flora, fauna, and other natural resources being maintained and preserved for future generations.

Holy mountains have a special value that makes them worth protecting at all costs. Beliefs and attitudes held by people who revere them can function as powerful forces which serve to preserve the integrity of natural environments, and thereby help promote conservation, restore damaged environments and strengthen indigenous cultures. For instance, Indian scientists have been working with Hindu priests at the Badrinath shrine in the Himalayas to encourage pilgrims to plant seedlings for reasons connected to their religious and cultural traditions. They hold planting ceremonies that allow people to enrich their pilgrimage experience by restoring an ancient sacred forest. Likewise, as KMY yatris, each one of us was encouraged to plant a seedling in a pre-selected patch of degraded forest at Gunji, called the 'Manasarovar Van'. In order to be sustainable over the long term, environmental policies and programmes need to take such values and ideals into account; otherwise, they will fail to enlist the local and popular support that they need to succeed.

3

Must-See Places En-route

Routes to places having irresistible appeal, which have been documented and drawn systematically by modern-day travellers, interestingly are not found delineated pin-pointedly in the available ancient literature in the Kailas-Manasarovar pilgrimage. These two holy places receive extensive descriptions and references in *Ramayana* of Valmiki and *Mahabharata* and *Puranas* (mythological texts and sub texts) of Veda Vyas. A sizable body of ancient literature exists in relation to Kailas-Manasarovar and many other important tirthas.

In *Nandi Purana*, broad hints are found about paths that could be taken for trekking towards Kailas-Manasarovar. It is stated that ahead of the tri-junction after negotiating some distance from the Kedar region (केदार क्षेत्र), there are three paths that lead to Kailas. The first one proceeds towards Badrinath (or Vishnupur), the second one via Brahmapur and the third one straight to Kailas:

एकं विष्णुपुरं याति द्वितीयं ब्रह्मवेश्मनि।
कैलासमार्गं तृतीयं त्रिधा मार्गस्य लक्षणम्।।

Geographical boundaries of our national states drawn up in the middle of the twentieth century and political changes in the neighbourhood do not permit unfettered explorations of these three routes to Kailas-Manasarovar. It is also not possible for common pilgrims to withstand the adverse weather and geographical conditions in following the routes indicated in *Nandi Purana*. Pilgrimages without challenges and rigour, including due to the fury of nature, it is said rarely leave an indelible imprint on the mind. The *Nandi Purana* also indicates the most suitable period for undertaking them. The month of *Ashwin* (mid-September to mid-October) is stated to be the best time for the visit:

आश्विने मासे सम्प्राप्ते गन्तव्यं शंकरालयम्।

Resources and facilities available now-a-days did not exist in the distant past. It is hardly known that since the medieval period right until the 1962 unprovoked war China thrust upon India, in an unbroken tradition the Pal dynasty of Princely Askote State, which overlaps with present-day Pithoragarh district, took care of the arrangements, including board and lodging, of small groups of pilgrims who reached out to them. *Dharmsalas* (धर्म-शाला) and security detail through the Army of this Kingdom, had been set up along the trails, some known and others carved out by pilgrims themselves. It can, thus, be safely inferred that only a very few spiritually-committed seekers and sages would have had the wherewithal or courage to undertake the extremely arduous trek towards Kailas and take the holy dip in the icy waters of Manasarovar due to various information gaps, and adverse weather, topography and geographical conditions. The journey would take a much longer period to complete, if indeed that was the outcome.

It was but natural that these most-glorified destinations received the most determined and detached seekers for whom their lack of easy accessibility did not matter. The rarest of the rare yogis, who had the ability to control their body and mind, undertook the journey. It is for this reason the scriptures openly declared that without the blessing of Lord Shiva, it is not possible to pass through the treacherous highways enroute Kailas-Manasarovar:

विना रुद्रप्रसादेन न लभन्ते महापथम्।

Seekers pursuing the highways of spirituality and performing this pilgrimage were hardly interested in doing detailed documentation of the routes followed by them or of the places they took refuge in. However, those who undertook regular visits to Tibet in connection with trade and commerce, tourism, exploration, adventure, expansion of kingdom or administrative boundaries, etc. and incidentally visited Kailas-Manasarovar have also given broad indications about the routes and access points from different directions with hardly any insights from ancient texts.

It can be gleaned from historical and mythological accounts that the majority of access routes followed by sages and pilgrims for Kailas-Manasarovar in olden times were via Pithoragarh, Uttarkashi and Chamoli districts of Uttarakhand. Lipulekh, Limpia Lekh, New Dhura, Unta Dhura, Neeti, Mana and Nilang Pass also happened to be the known access points for trade and commerce in addition to pilgrimage before political borders were drawn with effective dominance of China over Tibet. In fact, it is said that prior to the 1962 war by China, as many as 18 access points were open for this pilgrimage through hilly terrains which form part of present-day Uttarakhand State, writes S.S. Pangati in his book- "*Shiva Bhumi Kailas*" (शिव भूमि कैलाश, पृ. 2). Late Swami Pranavanand has captured 12 routes in detail in his book "*Kailas-Manasarovar*".

Lalitaditya, King of Kashmir (699-735 AD) ruled over major parts of Tibet. Later on, in the year 1840 Gulab Singh, as King of Kashmir amalgamated Ladakh region of Tibet into his kingdom. Zoravar Singh, the courageous chief of his powerful Army, while on a visit to Kailas-Manasarovar in 1841 had set up his headquarters at Tirtha Puri near Mount Kailas. It was easier and distance shorter to reach Kailas-Manasarovar from Ladakh. That route is no more available due to adversarial neighbourhood and for political reasons.

After the Chinese aggression and intrusions into India in 1962, all the routes for Kailas-Manasarovar were closed by our northern ambitious neighbour. It was only in 1981, an agreement was signed between India and China which facilitated resumption of the pilgrimage albeit to a very limited number of Indians each year through Lipulekh Pass once again. The distance from Almora (Uttarakhand), the first night halt in the journey originating from New Delhi by road, to Kailas-Manasarovar is about the same as it is from New Delhi to Almora. Yet it takes 24 days (including 3 days of preparations in New Delhi) to perform it. It is an exalting and exciting experiment and experience to perform the adventurous pilgrimage via Lipulekh notwithstanding some amount of risks in trekking through difficult mountainous terrains and passes prone to land-slides.

Persuasive efforts by Government of India resulted in opening of one more route in the year 2015 to 10 batches, each one of 50 Indian pilgrims. This is via Nathula Pass in the State of Sikkim. The route traverses through the vast Tibetan Plateau. Though much longer in distance, it takes a lesser number of days (21 days, including 3 preparatory ones in New Delhi) due to the road infrastructure created by India and China on their respective side of the border. Those who wish to visit Kailas-Manasarovar via Kathmandu and Nathula Pass can thus reach there by road without physically trekking any distance except about 52 km circumambulation (परिक्रमा) of Mount Kailas. Those who travel via Kathmandu often finish the journey following the tour itinerary and mode of travel provided by their tour operator in less than two weeks.

The Uttarakhand route via the 5,335 metres (17,500 feet) high Lipulekh Pass connecting Pithoragarh with Tibet, which opened once again only in 1981, involved extensive trekking when I had undertaken it. Originating at New Delhi, pilgrims were initially transported by road to Dharchula and onward to Narayan Swami Ashram by jeep, from where the trek on foot for me (and on ponies for some) began. The yatra has been recently enhanced to 18 batches of a maximum of 60 yatris per batch coordinated and led by a Government-sponsored Liaison Officer. Now, in May 2020 with the opening of Link Road – Kailas-Manasarovar Yatra Route – providing road connectivity between Dharchula to Lipulekh Pass on the Indian side as well, pilgrims are likely to find the pilgrimage smoother and easier. But they may stand to miss out on unique and exhilarating experiences trekking through mountain vistas, which are at times harsh on the trekker and many-a-times sylvan and elevating.

The yatras are usually organized soon after snow melts sufficiently to enable traversing the Lipulekh Pass between the first week of June to until the end of September every year. People desirous to undertake the journey are required to make an online application in accordance with notified procedures and timelines. Termed the 'Kailas-Manasarovar Yatra (KMY)', the two official routes from India through the passes at Lipulekh or Nathula are strictly regulated by the Indian and Chinese Governments through the respective Ministries of External Affairs/ Foreign Affairs. For the smooth conduct of KMY, besides the Chinese authorities, the Indian side coordinates with various Indian agencies, notable ones being State Government of Uttarakhand, Indo-Tibetan Border Police (ITBP), and Kumaon Mandal Vikas

Nigam (KMVN). The more expensive leg of the journey through Tibet, now an autonomous region of China, is conducted under the active vigilance of Chinese Government through their designated agency.

On the Indian side, the Ministry provides assistance, on self-financing basis to selected yatris covering facilities like transport, accommodation, food, medical tests, guides, etc. Of late, some State Governments have begun providing financial support to pilgrims of their State. A thorough health check-up at Delhi in close association with medical wing of ITBP and Delhi Heart and Lung Institute seals the fate of the yatris to have the darshan of the abode of the Lord or to be declared ineligible on health grounds. A second check up at Gunji by ITBP's team of doctors just prior to cross-over at Lipulekh Pass has dashed the hopes of some – it almost did mine, but for my perseverance having been born and lived my entire childhood in the region. Any health problems of yatris occurring during the trek up to Gunji are addressed by an accompanying medical doctor of State Government of Uttarakhand and between Gunji and Lipulekh Pass by ITBP. Interestingly, delicious and nutritious local cuisine is arranged towards cooked meals by KMVN on both legs of the pilgrimage on Indian side along with darshan of local deities and cultural gatherings at places of night halt.

The period for common pilgrims and tourists to make trips to Kailas and Manasarovar via Kathmandu is also June to September when high mountain routes are navigable. This route despite entailing a much longer distance is considered relatively better by those who value physical and life-style comforts or those who do not win the auction under the official KMYs. Thus, the number of pilgrims and tourists opting for Kathmandu route through paid packages offered by private tourist agencies far exceeds those who travel via the Nathula and Lipulekh routes.

Manas Khand (मानस खण्ड) of Skanda Purana (स्कन्दपुराण) is seen glorifying this pilgrimage via Lipulekh. In its Chapter 11, the strenuousness of this journey has been explained while emphasizing that for pilgrims undertaking it with complete devotion, it is easy and pleasurable. According to the relevant description summarized below, Kurmachal mountain ranges in the northern part of India are very rich in terms of holy places and shrines, in addition to forests along with their wild species–

> *"It is auspicious to undertake this journey through these mountain ranges. In the beginning, pilgrims completely submerged in devotion are exhorted to take a holy bath in Lohawati and Gandaki rivers, visit shrines of Lord Shiva and other Gods and Goddesses in the vicinity, and offer prayers before the Kurma Shila at the banks of Sarayu river. Pilgrims should proceed to the Hansa Tirtha thereafter and take a dip in its holy waters. After this, they should cross the Daru Mountain to reach Patal Bhuvneshwar where they should observe fasting for two days and offer prayers with respectful devotion.*
>
> *After observing the requisite rituals at Patal Bhuvneshwar, devotees need to move ahead to again have a holy bath in river Ram Ganga followed by prayers of Lord Shiva and flocks in his service before proceeding towards Hansadhwaj mountain. After offering prayers with a pure heart on Hansadhwaj for Dhwajesh, pilgrims should proceed to reach the confluence of rivers Kali and Gori. Here, they should offer sincere prayers before Kaleesh.*
>
> *The confluence of Kali and Gori rivers is the entry point for Chaturdranst (Chaudas) mountain. Pilgrims should pay their respectful obeisance to this mountain, which is to be viewed as the teeth of Himalayas. After this begins the entry through Dharma-dwar in the Ashram of sage Vyasa. Devotees should*

offer prayers for sage Vyasa, the author of Mahabharata and eighteen Puranas.

According to sage Vashishtha, after offering prayers for sage Vyasa who is completely engrossed in transcendental meditation in this Ashram, which also happens to be the origin of mighty river Kali, there is no need for pilgrims to perform any further religious rituals during the remaining part of their journey. Pilgrims should, however, show respectful feelings towards local inhabitants in the same way as for sages and seers. They should also experience divinity within.

Having crossed Vyas ashrama, pilgrims should pray before the Goddess residing on Keral mountain while proceeding towards Puloman mountain. After meditating upon the deity Pulomesh residing in the centre of Puloma lake on the peak of Puloman mountain, devotees should enter into Tarak mountain. They should take a holy bath at the confluence of holy rivers Tarini and Sharada and pray in front of Tarakeshwar Shiva before moving towards Gauri mountain. After crossing Gauri mountain, pilgrims reach Manasarovar to feel a divine experience. Lord Shiva's presence is seen in Manasarovar in the form of a Raj Hansa or royal swan".

Important places enroute to Kailas-Manasarovar found and visited while undertaking the journey via Lipulekh Pass are extensively described in Manas Khand. It is, however, a subject of deeper research to correlate these places with the current local nomenclatures. The routes for the pilgrimage have been changing apace with refinements in connectivity and facilities created over time. Still, it is expected that inquisitive travellers will get interested in the significant places enroute mentioned in ancient texts.

Jageshwar or Jageeshwar

Known as a Jyotirlinga (ज्योतिर्लिंग) named "Nagesh" (नागेश) of Lord Shiva- "नागेशं दारुकावने", one of the twelve Sovereign Symbols (स्वयम्भू ज्योतिर्लिंग), this ancient shrine is situated inside one of the most attractive dense devadaru or pine (देवदारु) forests in lower Himalayas.

According to some claims, Lord Shiva in the form of Jyotirlinga Nagesh is located in Odha village near Hyderabad, State of Telangana or as some others claim about 20 km north-east of Dwarika, State of Gujarat. However, these claims are not rooted in ancient literature and religious geography nor can these be reconciled through visits to these places. Both leave no scope for any doubt or controversy in relation to actual location of Nagesh Jyotirlinga of Lord Shiva in Jageshwar. The climatic and geographical conditions of Hyderabad as well as of Dwarika are patently not conducive to the growth of Devadaru (pine) forests. This alone is sufficient to reject any such claim regarding the location of this Jyotirlinga in near Hyderabad or Dwarika. The word Daruka denotes Devadaru, and no other flora. Any other tree to be taken from the word "Daruka" will make the expression "दारुकावने" meaningless. In Sanskrit, a group of live trees is known as वन (forest).

Followers of Lord Shiva who believe that Jyotirlinga Nagesh is indeed situated near Dwarika seek to substantiate their claim by citing a story from Shiva Purana. A demon called Daruka had imprisoned the Brahmin sage Sukriya, who happened to be a great devotee of Lord Shiva. This dedicated devotee, while in prison established an idol of his beloved deity there. Daruka tries to kill Sukriya after hearing about this. Then, Lord Shiva appeared in human form to protect his devotee. Using his famous weapon Pasupathi

(पाशुपतास्त्र), he killed Daruka instantaneously. Thus, the symbol of Lord Shiva established by sage Sukriya became famous as one of the twelve Jyotirlingas known as 'Nagesh'. This narrative does not appear to be a convincing interpretation of the text in Shiva Purana notably since it tries to associate the Jyotirlinga, which is the Sovereign Symbol of Lord Shiva, with the demon Daruka.

It needs to be remembered that temples of Lord Shiva stand established in various parts of Indian sub-continent by his devotees. Mythological texts too mention many of these. But it would not be logical to conclude that every symbol or temple of Lord Shiva which finds mention in Puranas is one among the twelve Jyotirlingas. Take for instance the fact that there is hardly any tree cover in the place claimed to be the location of Nagesh Jyotirlinga near Dwarika, let alone Devadaru forests in any relatable vicinity. It is hardly natural to have a place named after a demon or a terrorist for one of the most famous shrines of Lord Shiva. On the contrary, a naturally well-endowed and beautiful place adorned by dense Devadaru forests in which sages and seers typically performed their meditation and reaching out to divinity personified could be a natural choice for the holy shrine of Lord Shiva. This is extensively supported by mythological narratives given below. The preference of Lord Shiva for the Himalayan region is hardly a secret.

In Prasad Mandapam (प्रसादमण्डपम्), an ancient text, this holy place in the lower Himalayas surrounded by dense forests of Devadaru is described as an abode of Lord Shiva:

हिमाद्रेरुत्तरे पार्श्वे देवदारुवनं परम्।
पावनं शंकरस्थानं तत्र सर्वे शिवार्चिताः।।

In Chapter 4 of Manas Khand, depiction of an interesting episode goes on to substantiate that Jageshwar is one of the most holy places from where distribution of the core organ of Lord Shiva worshiped in the form of Linga (लिंग) took place. The tale goes on to recount that the famous king Daksha Prajapati (दक्ष प्रजापति), father-in-law of Lord Shiva, organized a religious function called Yajna (यज्ञ) in his palace. Deliberately, he did not invite his daughter Sati and her husband Shiva to grace the function. Even after being dissuaded by Shiva on the grounds that there was no invitation from her father, Sati insisted to participate and went to her father's palace. She found herself humiliated personally and heard abusive invectives to describe her husband and his life-style. This became impossible for her to bear. Rather than going back to her husband, to lessen the impact of her humiliation she threw herself into the sacrificial fire and died. Hearing about the self-immolation by Sati, Shiva and his followers in outrage destroyed the place where Yajna was being performed. Lord Shiva carrying the partially-burnt body of his beloved Sati in his arms wandered across the universe for some time. Ultimately, a complete detachment from the world descended in him and he got engrossed in meditative practices in Daruka forest. After some time, Lord Shiva entered in the state of deep meditation or Samadhi (समाधि). At the same time, a group of seven sages, namely, Kashyap, Vashishth, Vishvamitra, Bharadwaj, Atri, Gautam and Jamadagni, were also residing with their respective spouse for meditative practices in Daruka forest.

One day, the wives of the sages suddenly saw the radiating Lord Shiva in the state of samadhi while they were collecting materials for offering an oblation with fire (हवन) to be performed by their husbands. Thunder-struck and spell-bound, the captivating influence of the Lord in Samadhi rooted them to the spot, and they became oblivious to the passage of time, their wifely duties, household chores and all else. When they did not return with the materials required for their rituals, the seven sages could not perform their oblation with fire, and got greatly worried. Having somehow spent the whole night in restless wait for their wives, they left in their search at dawn. After some wanderings, they found them in a trance with eyes singularly centred on Shiva who was in the deep state of meditation. They were blissfully unaware of happenings around. This scene was intolerable to the sages who lost their mental balance and perspective, and with that their power of discrimination. In seething rage, they cursed Lord Shiva although in samadhi, presuming that he had enticed their spouses in the act of faithlessness, each towards her husband. They cursed the Lord that the Shivalinga will disintegrate from his body and fall on land:

येन वै भवता योगिन् अस्माकं हि कुलस्त्रियः।
तस्माल्लिंगस्य पतनं तव भूमौ महेश्वर।।

Waking up from samadhi, Lord Shiva accepted the curse in spite of his innocence. He did not feel it appropriate to nullify the effect of their words spoken in curse. He informed them instead that his eyes, even when cast inimically on traitors and those guilty of killing their offspring and friends, liberates them. Thus, showing magnanimity in response to the curse, Lord Shiva liberated the seven sages to take the form of seven stars in a northerly direction of the sky, Sapta Rishi (सप्त ऋषि), in the era of next progenitor. However, the Sapta Rishi would remain without worldly enjoyments despite having the company of their spouses:

मत्तो मुक्तिं समालभ्य पत्नीभिः सह वै द्विजाः।
भोगहीनोत्तरस्यां हि भवध्वं दिवि तारकाः।।

In order to give meaning to the words of the seven sages spoken in curse, Lord Shiva caused the Shivalinga (शिवलिंग)

to fall on land, piercing the earth and reaching the last layer of the seven regions or worlds under the earth (पाताल). When the pain and weight became intolerable for earth, she went to Lord Vishnu for relief stating that she was not capable of bearing the entire weight of his Linga in one place. Lord Vishnu, along with Lord Brahma, proposed to break it in parts with the permission of Lord Shiva. Lord Shiva agreed and asked Lord Vishnu to use his Sudarshan Chakra (सुदर्शन चक्र), the circular sharp-edged missile weapon, for the task and to establish the pieces of Shivalinga in nine regions of the earth – the Himalayas, Manas, Kailas, Kedar, Patal, Kashi, Reva, Brahmottar, and Nagar (हिमाद्रि, मानस, कैलाश, केदार, पाताल, काशी, रेवा, ब्रह्मोत्तर तथा नागर). And thus, the all-pervasiveness of the Shivalinga is demystified. Needless to say, that Jageshwar area forms part of the Himalayas or हिमाद्रि. This story, unlike that of demon Daruka, adds credence to the location of a unique Jyotirlinga in Ardhanareeshwar (अर्ध-नारीश्वर) form of "Nagesh" at Jageshwar.

In Chapter 61 of Manas Khand, importance of Jageshwar tirtha has been emphasized. It is stated that pilgrimage to the shrine of Lord Shiva in the holy place surrounded by dense pine (Devadaru) forests, situated in the southern side of river Sarayu offers benefits equal to performing an Ashvamedha Yajna (a Vedic religious ritual in which a horse is sacrificed). It is underlined that in this Darukavana (दारुकावन), Lord Shiva remains awake all the time in the form of Nagesh or Nageswara. His symbol, the Jyotirlinga of this holy place, is the genesis of symbols or Shivalingas in other places. Jageshwar is the local name for Nageswara. A number of mountains in lower Himalayas in the vicinity of Jageshwar are known as Karakotak Nag, Kali Nag, Dhauli Nag, Pheni Nag, Beri Nag, Vasuki Nag, Pingal Nag, etc. The presiding deity of a mountain

(नग) in the local lexicon is Nag (नाग). None other than Lord Shiva in the name of Nagesh or Nageswara is the highest among them.

Jageshwar, situated 40 km from Almora on the Almora-Pithoragarh highway, has 125 ancient big temples and miniatures. These include the main temples of Jageshwar, Mrityunjaya, Pushti Devi, Navadurga, Navagrih, Sun, etc. It is matter of deeper historical research as to how, and exactly when, these archaeological marvels were created. According to local lore, renovation of these temples was done during the rule of King Shalivahana. Many say that the temples were constructed by Kings of Katyuri belonging to the Chandravanshi (lunar) dynasty between eighth and fourteenth century AD.

A key feature of this Jyotirlinga is that it appears divided in two parts. The larger part is identified with Lord Shiva and the smaller on the left with Goddess Parvati, his beloved. In other words, this Jyotirlinga in Jageshwar represents him as Ardhanareeshwara or a composite androgynous form – totality that lies beyond duality.

It is also to be understood here that tales narrated in the Puranas are not necessarily to be taken for their literal meaning. They could be symbolic as well as hyperbolic, their aim being to attract the attention of all manner of persons through catchy and interesting characterisations designed to convey the core substantive that is existing in an abstract form. These tales were thus means of communication intended to reach all such common men who were not able to internalize the abstract as an abstract. There could be an adverse fall out of such characterisations as well, with some others finding the depiction of the lofty abstract reduced to a simplistic substantive inconsistent with the deeper interpretations of ancient scriptures.

In the year 1995, the Archaeological Survey of India established a museum near Jageshwar temples. It was renovated in the year 2002. This beautiful museum has a rare collection of 160 idols dating back to eighth to fourteenth centuries AD. The rare idols along with other artifacts had been recovered from Jageshwar and places around. They have been exhibited meaningfully in the galleries of the museum which has increased footfall and made it extremely attractive and popular with visitors.

Pilgrims and travellers who undertake the official KMY are offered an opportunity to visit the Jageshwar shrines and the Museum on the return journey to Delhi.

Patal Bhuvneshwar

Situated near Hat Kalika Shakti Peeth (हाट-कालिका शक्ति पीठ) in Pithoragarh district, Patal Bhuvneshwar (पाताल) is an important set of caves that can be visited by taking a short detour from Berinag, Chaukori or Almora on the official yatra. According to a mythological story, when there were no rains for twelve years on earth leading to famine, the great seer Bhrigu came with his disciples from the banks of river Reva to the Himalayas. On the way, hearing about these spiritually vibrant holy caves of Patal Bhuvneshwar, he set up a hermitage nearby. He demystified the secrets, attributes and holiness of the caves to his disciples, engaged in meditative practices, along with their importance for pursuing the path of meditation.

When and how the huge underground caves of Patal Bhuvneshwar were created remains a mystery till date. The series of caves are said to be linked to each other deep underground, with all but the one now seen naturally closed to mankind one by one with the passage of time. In Chapters 103-104 of Manas Khand, there is a detailed description of

Patal Bhuvneshwar. This holy place situated between rivers Sarayu and Ram Ganga is an integral part of Daruka mountain. He who wants to feel the presence of eternal power should come to the sacred Patal Bhuvneshwar situated near the confluence of rivers Ram Ganga and Sarayu. Many renowned seers, including sage Vashishtha, had been inhabiting in this place, which was also preferred for meditation by various Gods and Goddesses to serve and please Lord Shiva. Thirty-three crore or thirty-three classes of Gods and Nagas living in Patal or regions below the earth lighted this place variously to propitiate Lord Vishnu who enhanced the beauty of Patal Bhuvneshwar by inhabiting there. There are plenty of jewels illuminating this place, offered by the mystical and fabulous King of Serpents, Sheshanag (शेषनाग), who resided in Patal:

सरयूरामयोर्मध्ये पातालभुवनेश्वरः।
शेषनागेनदत्तानि रत्नान्यश्वश्च कामग।।

It is said that seekers with faith and devotion coming to these caves get benefits millions of times higher than those derived by visiting Kashi and Setubandh Rameshwar; thousands of times more than what is attained by pilgrimage to Kedarnath (केदारनाथ); and a thousand times more benefits than from an Ashwamedha Yajna, concludes Manas Khand. It is believed to be the holiest place on earth.

The glory of Lord Shiva living in Patal Bhuvneshwar is sung by Yakshas (यक्ष), Gandharvas (गन्धर्व), Vidyadharas (विद्याधर), and Apsaras (अप्सरा). He is worshiped by all Gods and Goddesses. Paeans of praise are sung continuously by all supernatural creatures. This holy place is also liked by Goddess Parvati for her relaxation, in addition to being the preferred place of other Gods. Brahma is stated to frequent this place to have an audience with Lord Shiva, who lives here awake forever. The caves are also believed to have an underground passage connecting them to Mount Kailas.

The natural beauty of Patal Bhuvneshwar can also be seen from a geographical point of view. Large-sized Devadaru trees adorn this place situated at a distance of about 150 km from Almora on the highway leading to Pithoragarh, which is about 70 km from the caves. Before arriving here, one reaches a village called Bhuvneshwar. Just below this village are a number of ancient temples named Vriddh Bhuvneshwar, which house idols of many deities. A very old, albeit broken, idol of Lord Shiva with Parvati is seen in the compound. The ancient Chandrika temple on the southern side houses the idol of Lord Shiva in the form of Ardhanareeshwara. By its side is an idol of a Goddess with eight hands made of 8 metals – Ashtadhatu (अष्ट-धातु). The Goddess in an aggressive posture with weapons in her hands, namely, mace, sword, trident, and javelin, appears to be prepared to fight to the finish with demons. The main temple was constructed in the twelfth century AD by Chand and Katyuri kings. The famous caves appearing to be super natural is 5 km away from this temple.

After scientific examinations of rocks and stones, geologists estimate the cave formation to about 5,100 years old. It is inferred that river Ram Ganga was flowing nearby, into which a number of water fountains and rivulets originating from the hills in vicinity merged. River Bhargavi flowing by the side seems to be testifying to this reality of the distant past. The caves inside present pictures of a number of mythological narratives as if carved carefully by expert artists conversant with the culture, religion and mythology of the distant past.

The main entrance to the cave is known as Dharma-Dwar (धर्म-द्वार). According to local lore, the cave has three more entry points, which were closed one-by-one in different time zones. A story is legion that Paap-Dwar (पाप-द्वार) to the left of Dharma Dwar was closed after the death of Ravana in Treta Yuga (त्रेता युग). Similarly, Rana-Dwar (रण-द्वार) to the right was closed after Mahabharata in Dwapar Yuga (द्वापर युग). The fourth access point called Moksha-Dwar (मोक्ष-द्वार) had already been closed at the end of Sata Yuga (सत युग).

On the rocks inside the cave, many narratives of Ramayana, Mahabharata and Puranas have been exhibited through natural physiological formations and structures. It may be difficult for those who have not read ancient literature to internalize all the wonderful descriptions and mysteries carved out in its rock formations. Even so, even a layman cannot remain unimpressed after seeing with one's gross eyes the wonders inside this super-natural cave.

Immediately after descending down about 90 feet from the cave's mouth, the main entrance, to the floor, one finds the fabulous serpent-king Sheshanag expanding his huge hoods and holding the whole earth on his head. Little ahead of that is a fire hole (हवन कुण्ड) where King Janmejaya (the descendent of Pandavas) performed Yajna to sacrifice the serpent called Takshak (तक्षक), the killer of his father. The picture of Vasuki Nag is also seen in the vicinity. After moving forward, one finds the headless body of Ganesa, the son of Lord Shiva and Parvati. The pictures of Badrinath, Kedarnath and Amarnath could also be seen nearby. All the four holy places (चार धाम) can be seen in pictorial depictions inside the cave.

Inside this massive main cave, there are many segments containing smaller caves which include three famous ones – Sumeru, Samar, and Sudama. It is said that sage Markandeya with many others had performed meditation inside these caves for a long time. Just below one of the smaller caves, the fifth head of Brahma separated from his body is found which is known as Brahmakapali (ब्रह्म-कपाली). Just above it is Kamdhenu (कामधेनु) with milk flowing from her udders.

Except homage (तर्पण) to ancestors, no other ritual is performed here. There is a tiny water body inside the cave. Usage of its water is prohibited according to local belief. Not very far from here are pictures of the long-matted hairs of Lord Shiva in milky and black colours. It is said that Bhagirathi river remains hidden in them. The space behind them is occupied by 33 koti demi-gods who are there to offer their dedicated services to propitiate Lord Shiva. The picture of sage King Bhagirath is also seen by the side of Nandi (नन्दी) and Bhringi (भृंगी) who form the chariot of Lord Shiva. At a distance, the sky with its galaxy including the group of seven stars can be seen. In front of the galaxy is the majesty of Lord Shiva on a copper plate, in the centre of which are the three symbols (त्रिलिंग) of Brahma, Vishnu and Shiva. River Ganga flowing from the top is seen sprinkling water on them. On the wall below are three pictures statedly of Brahma, Vishnu and Shiva. There are innumerable symbols and pictures in there; it is not possible to offer details here.

Jageshwar Temples and Patal Bhuvneshwar Caves

Jageshwar amidst Devadaru - *Jyotirlinga of Ardhanareeshwara*

Patal Bhuvneshwar Cave Entrance, Vriddh Bhuvneshwar

Sub-terranean super-natural: Adishesha, Kund, Shiva's Tresses

First Flush of Himalayan Odyssey

Glimpses of nature

River Kali at Dharchula and in Chaudas Valley

Narayan Swami Ashram and Vishnu Narayan, the presiding deity

Challenging Trek - Narayan Swami Ashram to Gunji

Breath-taking Glimpses of Nature around Sirakha

Jungle Chatti to Gala, quite exhilarating with ferocious river Kali along side narrow treacherous staircases

Some more treacherous pathways to Budhi

River Kali, in symphony with waterfalls and streams

River Kali, in symphony with waterfalls and streams

4

A Journey Within Begins Here

Towards Narayan Swami Ashram

The first leg of the journey to Kailas-Manasarovar originates from New Delhi at dawn with pooja and chanting for a successful darshan of Lord Siva in his high abode. A most fulsome felicitation of yatris followed by sumptuous breakfast marks a ceremonial send-off at Ghaziabad by voluntary organisations and private persons who support the yatra of each batch of yatris. After negotiating a distance of about 300 km, the first significant halt is at Kathgodam. This journey by road is in comfortable air-conditioned coaches, although there exists a better option to travel by train that takes less time. Perhaps status quo has been maintained from times when road was the only option.

After lunch at the Tourist Rest Centre (TRC), KMVN and some formalities which include felicitation of pilgrims in accordance with the local traditions by local people, the journey proceeds with the first night halt at TRC Almora by travelling another 90 km through the hills. Enroute the first spiritual halt, albeit quite brief, is at the Baba Neem Karoli Ashram, Kainchi Dham near Bhowali. On reaching Almora, this cultural capital of Kumaon lays out its delicious local cuisine and heart-warming cultural embrace for the pilgrims. A variety of songs and musical items on folklore which has been passed from generation to generation in oral tradition are presented by colourful troupes in their regalia. This is much more than an evening's simple entertainment.

On leaving Almora, there is a brief darshan, this time of the hugely popular Chitai Golu Devata. The Mandir is strung with thousands of bells each seeking a devotee's ardent wish fulfilment. Travel through Bageshwar at the confluence of rivers Sarayu and Gomati ends at Dharchula with a lunch break at Chaukori from where one could enjoy a fantastic view of snow-topped western Himalayan range.

The entire journey unfolds the beauty of nature, rich in flora and fauna, with the road curving and criss-crossing through ever-changing landscapes of lush green hills and valleys, gorges, and ravines, which play hide and seek with meadows full of wild-flowers and woodlands with trees standing tall as though aiming for the clear blue sky.

Colours of local culture and receptions of pilgrims at Chaukori and Meerthi once again convey the warmth of local communities. At Meerthi, ITBP briefs the yatris on the journey ahead, cautioning against taking risks while trekking, and safeguarding against high altitude sickness.

After crossing Askote and Jauljibi, about 30 km before Dharchula and where river Gori meets river Kali is a sight to behold and is a harbinger of the unfolding divine beauty of nature in mountains and valleys. Traversing the hills and valleys by road, pilgrims are increasingly exposed to Himalayan ecology including a number of rivers, namely, Sarayu, Gomati, Ramganga, Dhauli, Gori, and Kali, with their dancing tributaries and playful waterfalls. Himalayan ranges present the diverse ecology and raw earthy beauty which defies words.

Dharchula, the next night halt, is on the banks of river Kali with Nepal on the other side. Logistics undergo a sea change here; baggage rules and restrictions come into operation. Each yatri is required to carry 5 kg of common foodstuff for the batch for use on Tibetan leg of yatra. Personal luggage in excess of 20 kg is not allowed. Lockers to store excess (and usables for return journey) are provided by KMVN. Yatris also hire their pony and/or personal porter for both onward and return legs of the trek on Indian side between Narayan Swami Ashram and Lipulekh. Every need is to be anticipated and tied up. Given sparce population and bare-bone amenities at transit food camps and night halts, wisdom lies in tying up pony-porter needs in advance. These needs are then tied up by KMVN for the entire batch, under oversight of Liaison Officer, at Dharchula. There is also an element of providing valuable employment to the youth who offer such services during the summer break from their studies. Not quite a quid-pro-quo for the generous voluntary welcomes and hospitality of local population, it is a graceful way for yatris to give productive strength to a remote region where alternatives to agricultural occupations are rare and hardly developed.

The journey advances through Chaudas valley offering plenty of unseen telling surprises as if natural divinity is manifesting itself gradually. The 20 km stretch from Dharchula to Tawaghat, the confluence of Kali and Dhauli rivers, is full of excitement on a narrow road passing along with the shores of river Kali. From Tawaghat pilgrims reach Kanchoti or Chirkala village by covering a distance of about 6 km by road with river Dhauli by the side. For some time, river Kali disappears from sight. Pangu, a peaceful village about 20 km away from Tawaghat is unaffected by the sounds of forcefully-flowing rivers, Dhauli and Kali. These mighty rivers are invisible from this big village, which is the centre of Chaudas valley. Chhiplakot mountain ranges in the west and mountains of Nepal in the east present wonderful valley vistas, sometimes with sheer drops and at others soothing gentleness. After traversing another 13 km, pilgrims have the pleasure of entering Narayan Ashram, from where the trek on foot or by pony ride begins.

Tiredness and nausea associated with steeply-curving roads that might be felt by some pilgrims disappears with their arrival at Narayan Swami Ashram. The Ashram offers a sublime experience of nature and spiritual vibrations. Villages ahead after crossing Dharchula convey the simplicity, innocence and intrinsic generosity of local inhabitants who are mostly tribal. They form part of Chaudas valley or Vyas Valley. While the mighty river Kali with its ferocious sound and fury is seen demonstrating its fearsome might continuously, the snow-capped Himalayan ranges at some distance represent the most graceful and elevating face of the nature attracting attention of the pilgrims. The environment offers glimpses of nature in its purest and cleanest form inviting curiosity among inquisitive pilgrims who do not seem to feel any adverse affects of the strenuous trek as experience of bliss overtakes their mind.

Narayan Swami, his Ashram and Contributions

A marvellous mix of ancient and modern architecture, the Narayan Swami Ashram situated between two main villages- Sausa and Sirkha - symbolises the purity, energy and spirituality of the Himalayas. Established by one of the greatest saints of the twentieth century, this Ashram situated at an altitude of 2,734 metres (8,970 ft.) has been serving not only saints, devotees, and pilgrims who frequent Kailas-Manasarovar, but also as a centre contributing to the socio-economic development of villages situated in the region, in particular the remote parts bordering Tibet in the north and Nepal in the east. Surrounded by pine (Devadaru) forests and snow-covered Himalayas slashed multiple times by river Kali, this Ashram started to come into being in the year 1936 when there were no roads beyond Almora.

Details of Paramahansa Narayana Swami prior to his transcending to sainthood are not well documented. The limited available correspondence between him and his followers and information collected and collated by the latter suggest that he was born to a reputed Brahmin family in Bengaluru, and named Raghavendra. From a very early age, he started developing an acute sense of detachment towards worldly comforts and got attracted to the devotional path. He studied and got a degree in applied science from a reputed educational institution, but the call of holy places was strong and, in the process, come in contact with a number of sages. He moved to the spiritually-charged ambience of the Himalayas. One section of his followers believes his year of birth to be 1906 while another hold that it was actually 1914. There is an old adage that the "place, date of birth and age do not define sages". Narayan Swami who remained forever submerged in devotional bliss symbolized this adage in flesh and blood. He was physically tall and fair-complexioned with a wide bright forehead. He was quite young, when around the year 1934-35 his reputation as a visionary saint got established far and wide.

Narayan Swami had performed the Kailas-Manasarovar pilgrimage in 1935 along with another highly self-realized saint Ramananad Swami even though they did not have the requisite material resources for such a trip. Their journey started from the Dron Giri mountain in Almora. He had become quite weak physically after this arduous pilgrimage. On return, he stayed in the border village of Garbyang. People of Garbyang and peripheral villages took care of him and he too dedicated his entire life in their service and other remote villages in every possible way.

It is no secret that the pre-Independence colonial administration neglected remote areas inhabited by aboriginal communities. Simultaneously, it prevented movement of general population and extension of general administration to these areas. However, they facilitated penetration of Christian missionaries to such areas in the name of famine relief, education, and welfare programmes to implement their hidden agenda of converting innocent people inhabiting such areas to Christianity. One of them had opened a well-equipped Health Centre in Sirkha village, besides extending other facilities. No doubt the missionaries implemented some welfare measures and extended medical facilities in a limited way, but beneficiaries had to convert to be eligible for receiving the assistance. Those not willing to be thus induced had to remain deprived of the charity being extended by them. The virgin hinterland in Himalayan region from north to north-east and central India which were populated by aboriginals got saturated with missionary organizations quietly engaged in promoting their proselytization programmes with the active support of the then colonial masters. The cool climes of Himalayas, which were largely inaccessible except on foot, lacked even basic facilities for education, public health, etc., coupled with remoteness to others, ideally suited their agenda.

Narayan Swami wandering through the Himalayan villages might have noticed the lack of guile among locals being leveraged by wily missionaries. He lived in many a remote village to understand the needs of the people. He traversed many other villages far and wide with his team singing devotional songs and reciting of names of the Lord of Universe. Devotional songs and recitations or *Naam*

Samkeertan (नाम-संकीर्तन) were merely the primary tools of his avocation to assimilate these marginalized groups. By telling educative stories to elders, participating in cultural functions, and promoting sports and literacy among youngsters, he tried to break social taboos, superstitions and isolation of local communities. He succeeded in attracting and encouraging the illiterate locals towards education and inculcating ethical values in their lives.

Soon enough he got engaged in their actual integration with the mainstream of society. He started opening health and educational institutions, including hostels, to meet their basic needs which got expanded gradually. Swamiji also created cultural and literary consciousness and invoked pride in their ancient heritage by addressing gatherings regularly. His multi-dimensional activities and institution-building became an effective counter to inducements offered by proselytizing Christian missionaries. He became a household name in no time, and his work is remembered fondly and respectfully even today.

Name and fame, however, never distracted him from his spiritual path. The tenets of Sanatan Dharma propagated by him and its flag hoisted by aboriginal communities in remote Himalayan villages can be seen by visitors. He did not mobilize local people on the grounds of religion. Neither was he driven by any hidden agenda. His respect for the followers of Christian faith is evident from the fact that he opened a Christian school at Bageshwar. Probably, such examples are rare elsewhere.

In order to minimize the difficulties of saints and pilgrims visiting Kailas-Manasarovar, in addition to serving local communities, Swamiji decided to establish an Ashram or a centre of service on the banks of river Kali Ganga in Chaudas valley. In February-March of the year 1936, Swamiji, his brother saint Ramanand who was also a disciple of his Guru, and a lady saint Ruma Devi initiated steps for the construction of a hut in Sausa village about 60 km from Dharchula. As the site selected for the Ashram was found to be unsuitable, it was shifted to Kulauk village with the active support and desire of the local people.

The foundation stone of what became Narayan Swami Ashram with time was laid on 20 March 1936 in Kulauk village envisaging a wooden structure and thatched roof. People from nearby villages also participated in the foundation-laying ceremony in a big way singing devotional songs and chanting prayers, besides performing dances. Recognising its susceptibility to damage from hazards like fire, it was replaced by a fire-proof stronger structure, the construction of which started in the year 1939. In spite of lack of resources and absence of motorized transportation of construction materials, non-availability of expert masons and carpenters, the locals supported by the Nepalese from across river Kali participated energetically to contribute human and material capital and with an enthusiasm worthy of the determination shown by the visionary Swamiji.

Paved roads did not exist beyond Almora in those days. Even in the wider local area, there was no ready expertise available for the construction of a good building. Construction materials like cement, steel, bricks and mortar needed to be brought as head-loads of people or using ponies all the way from Almora, a distance of about 250 km from the Ashram's proposed site. Overcoming financial and other constraints that could have made the project a non-starter, things started falling in line slowly but surely, and with the addition of an expert Sikh mason from Bageshwar who volunteered to dedicate his services, a construction marvel was created in this remote location.

The grand Ashram with an imposing eye-catching appearance is built on a grassy table-top devoid of tree cover, which is overlooked by snow-capped Himalayan peaks on the one side presenting a unique and unparalleled natural beauty. On its eastern side at a distance of 3 km sparkle the rippling waters of ferociously-flowing river Kali which incidentally defines our borders with neighbouring Nepal. The recent political rift about the notification by Nepal of its extended borders to include the farthest tributary of the river Kali within its territory appears so needless, as though instigated, and utterly baseless when viewed from the prism of a collaborative past to the highest common creative and spiritual cause, such as at Narayan Swami Ashram, among the peoples of our two nations. On the western side of the Ashram, Chhipala Kedar impress all with its greenery from June to October and its snow-cover thereafter. Panch Chuli mountain ranges along side offer immense pleasure to the wonderstruck eyes of nature lovers. Swamiji's Ashram seem to unify its spiritual founder with nature, particularly during sunrise and sunset.

The grand statue of Vishnu Narayan, as if divinity sitting in blood and flesh, was installed in August 1946 which preceded large-scale cultural functions, congregations, recitations of devotional songs by villagers of Chaudas and Vyas valleys in groups with spontaneous participation. Two beautiful idols made of black stone donated by the Rajavar of Askote were placed in front the throne adorned by the Statue of Vishnu Narayan made of eight metals (अष्ट-धातु). These two idols were brought from Daradi temple situated deep inside the dense forests of Garjia Valley.

In the initial days Narayan Swami and his brother saint Ramanand Swami used to stay at the Ashram in solitude. Activities increased when Kailas-Manasarovar pilgrims started frequenting the Ashram. For long since then, the Ashram with its serene atmosphere has been attracting the attention of holy men, pilgrims and general tourists in addition to guiding the local population and contributing to their socio-economic well-being, directly and indirectly. It is a reminder of the great works done by these great Bhakti Yogi saints who felt bliss, as much in deep meditation and devotional songs as in serving humanity, particularly the poor in neglected far reaches of hinterland Uttarakhand with complete involvement as well as detachment. I was fortunate to spend some time in this Ashram on the way to Kailas-Manasarovar. My elder brother had studied in a school founded by Narayan Swami.

It is the magnetic effect of Swami's personality, serendipity, and serenity of the place that people inhabiting villages in Chaudas and Vyas valley continue to bear the flags of our most ancient cultural heritage. They continue to follow the path laid down for them by Swamiji. Local festivals celebrated with grandeur in these valleys include those in the memory of sage Vyas and Pandavas. Suffice to say that Christian zealots and colonial rulers did not succeed in their mission in this area in the same degree as elsewhere in the country. The Himalayan environment here continues to remain as vibrant today as it was in the distant past. Swamiji remains alive in the memory of local people. They continue to sing and pray reciting the names of Narayan (नाम-संकीर्तन) individually as well as in groups, more so on festive occasions and anniversaries, till date.

The Ashram and facilities there have expanded in course of time with increasing footfall. Built on trust and empathy, it provided safe drinking water to villages, promoted health and hygiene and worked towards elimination of superstitions without hurting the sentiments of locals. Marking a rare feat in those days, a drinking water project for Sosa was implemented under the direct supervision of Swamiji. Swamiji played cricket and other games with small children with noses that flowed faster than the river Kali and even lived amidst them in the most inhospitable conditions. Besides identifying with the local community, he sponsored both education and skill development of those in formative years in far-off places. He had the incredible ability to organize villagers whose trust and complete support were his proven strength. Some of the notable health and educational facilities opened by this visionary saint are the following:

- Bapu Mahavidyalaya, Narayan Nagar
- Upper Primary School, Jayakot
- Shrinarayan Harijan Pathshala, Chhaliachhiyaso
- Junior High School, Pangu
- Shasta Medical Home, Sosa
- Tapovan Travelling Dispensary
- Aryasamaj Anathashram Vidyalaya
- Sanskrit Pathashala, Kamedi Devi
- Christian School, Bageshwar
- Hostel, Kanda School
- Junior High School, Deval Thal
- Nanda Devi Upper Primary School, Jadapani
- Badarnath Dharamshala
- X-Ray Facility, Government Hospital, Pithoragarh

With foundations rooted strongly in spirituality and socio-cultural ethos of its environs, the Ashram will continue to remind posterity about the immeasurable contributions of Swamiji besides benefitting devout and visitors through spiritually-vibrant environment for times to come.

A combination of Bhakti Yoga and Karma Yoga in the human form, Paramahansa Narayan Swami was a highly detached and evolved soul despite appearing greatly attached towards socio-economic development of the downtrodden. For him serving the poor and realization of God were two sides of the same coin. Suddenly and quietly, he left the Ashram without informing other inmates or anyone in July 1954. His heath condition had been deteriorating for some time although he never discussed the matter with anyone in the Ashram or elsewhere. He was suffering from cancer; doctors had failed to diagnose the causes of his deteriorating health early enough. Before leaving the Ashram, Swamiji had ruled out the possibility of his return to the place again.

Two years later on 9 September 1956, inmates in the Ashram received information that Swamiji had demitted his physical form in a private nursing home in Kolkata. It is said that while wandering in the Himalayas, he had been grievously injured when he slipped into a deep trench. A piece of wood had pierced his thigh and lay struck there. This injury transformed into malignancy with the passage of time. Swamiji did not go to doctors or to hospitals in cities for treatment and there were no advanced hospitals and nursing facilities in the local area.

In a real sense, Swamiji immortalized himself through his services and spiritual endeavours. Gaiety and divinity of the Ashram and Vishnu Narayan temple remain a memorial to tell that an angel was sent by God from heaven in the form of a sage with a human body. Swami Pranavanand dedicated his famous book Kailas-Manasarovar published in the year 1949 to this great saint for his devoted work not only in the field of spirituality but also for his contributions in the socio-cultural development of the simple and smiling people of this region.

Chaudas and Vyas Valleys

The journey from Narayan Swami Ashram to Lipulekh

through the beautiful Chaudas valley and then Vyas valley is fraught with risks and adventures that shake the fainthearted, but also provides plentiful marvels and delights that touch the soul adding fillip to ones resolve to press on. It includes treks with measured steps, firm-footed and in stealth up and down steep slopes to move forward. Any loss of momentary attention while walking on the narrow rough rock-cut pathways alongside the forceful distractions and noise of river Kali as it flows downwards could be fatal.

However, the same trek becomes enjoyable with due care, discipline and respect for nature which keeps on expressing itself in various forms and manifestations. In that case, the fearsome noise and flow of the river is utterly musical imparting meditative strength to yatris on their inward journey to Lord Shiva. Tributaries, streams, waterfalls, rivulets merging themselves in this great river in different places seem to personify lovers eager to meet their beloved. With their rhythmic dance and musical choir, they become part of the river Kali adding to her force and sound as though in crescendo orchestrated by the unseen Lord. Singing birds and smiling flora and fauna, appearance of never-melting snow peaks, slopes without vegetative growth, flowering meadows, villages with ground subsidence below one's feet and rifts sheltering desolated, tilted houses, present the nature spanning the creative to the destructive full cycle. The fragility of Himalayan ecology is manifest in multiple landslides and broken and blocked pathways that were trod by sages and seers, what to speak of yatris before us. The nature also appears to be conveying a loud and clear message that respectful relationship with her offers blissful coexistence, but taking her for granted with any excessive or outrageous behaviour could lead to unthinkable misery and destruction.

From an environmental perspective, this phase of the journey offers first hand experience of an environment which is serene and largely free from pollution. Pilgrims start increasingly to breathe in clean mountain air. After getting recharged in the vibrant spirituality of Narayan Ashram for some time, this phase of journey gives options to pilgrims either to trek on foot or hire a pony and porter for support for the onward journey.

Sirkha at an altitude of 2,560 metres (8,400 ft.), 6 km from Narayan Ashram, is the next place for night halt. Facilities provided by KMVN are adequate. Inadequacies are more than compensated by nature's bounty.

The trekking of 16 km that starts next morning is full of patches with ups and downs. The initial 6 km to Rungling Top (at 3,048 metres) looks a bit strenuous though there is hardly any cause for scare or nervousness. Small habitations meet and greet the yatris with openness and warmth through gestures, diversities in nature and sites to draw attention, hardly allow them to feel exhausted.

Simthola village is about 5 km from Rungling Top. Another 5 km long trek from here takes the pilgrims to Gala at 2,440 metres, a scheduled halt. Peaks of Himalayas, waterfalls, streams dancing to rhythms unheard by human ear, diversity of plants and wild species, birds and animals, continuously enhance the curiosity and enrich the travellers, researchers, botanists, geologists, and anthropologists, in multiple ways. Trekking here is exhilarating and memorable.

After spending the night at Gala, the next leg springs more breath-taking wonders, adventures and surprises. After trekking 3 km from Gala, the mighty river Kali appears in sight at Jipti or Vindalakoti. However, one has to climb down 4,444 irregular stairs hewn in mountain-side rocks and stretching over about 2½ km to reach Lakhanpur (locally called Lakwar Phu). Even though small streams, waterfalls and quaint houses with artistic facades carved out in wood continue to engage pilgrims deeply and constantly, walking this stretch requires utmost care and attention. A distraction or momentary loss of balance of the yatri could mean sudden disappearance for all the times.

The trek from Lakhanpur to Budhi is quite narrow and treacherous, going past Khan Dera and Najyang all the way to reach Malpa. Yatris move upstream with caution as river Kali displays her ferocious form by relentlessly pounding rocks and shaking massive stone boulders as though it's a child's play.

The force of Kali appears to convey a message that any attempt to outrage her modesty is fraught with unpredictable risks and devastating outcomes. For those finding the physical form of divinity in nature, this river represents the pure love of a selfless mother in the form of fast-flowing stream of milk without discrimination. Rightly said, our creations are based upon our perceptions. Sages and seers wandering in the Himalayas and moving around holy places situated in the most inhospitable conditions survived blissfully as they internalized this divinity in nature. They did not worry about their sustenance requirements when nature's bounty opened its doors for them. That is how the highest philosophical thoughts conveying eternal truth presented by them based upon their experiences continue to be revered till date. It is but natural for those indulging in evil and malicious thoughts and exploitative intentions getting scared and feeling threatened by the mighty rivers, intimidating mountains, and vast ocean depths.

It is thus expected that travellers remain respectful towards the nature while moving ahead, and do nothing that could affect their concentration or fragile ecological balance. They can experience the bliss in the lap of nature only with a pure mind and heart. It was on this trek in the year 1998 at Malpa, the whole group of about 55 pilgrims lost their lives to a massive cloudburst and landslides which also rained rocks on them in a dense dark night. The entire village vanished without any trace. Malpa on the banks of river Kali has since after this tragedy no longer been earmarked as a place for night halt of pilgrims.

The confluence of river Budi and Kali near Malpa presents an intoxicating beauty for nature lovers. The milky waters of Budi on the one side and blackish-grey water of river Kali on the other offer paradoxical attributes in a pair of opposites. Their meeting and amalgamation seem to suggest that it is foolish to see contradictions in them, in deep love with each other. It is as if they were made for each other and meld seamlessly to present a common form. Together, they move and navigating around hindrances in perfect unison. Or it could be observed that river Budi with her smiling face and dancing postures was eager to break the seriousness visage of river Kali. The mountains behind river Budi look as if they are leaning down from the sky to bless her on the occasion of her blissful union with river Kali.

Starting at Gala, after negotiating a risky narrow trek of 18 km, Budhi village (at 2,680 metres, 8,890 ft.) is the next night halt. It also provides entry to Vyas valley. One cannot remain untouched by ecological changes during this journey. Enroute to Budhi, Lamari village holds special significance as the birthplace of Tyind Lama who settled in Budhi. Pilgrims are regaled with several myths about him; one calls him Phangt Lama (who could fly). Intrepid pilgrims can also rejoice in the hot springs said to have healing powers at Thakti, besides a beautiful waterfall at Kothla.

A steep climb of 3 km from Budhi leads to Chialekh (at 3,550 metres, 10,000 ft.). Chialekh grasslands, called 'Bugyal' locally, present nature in fantastic shades with a host of flowers all over the huge plains, with forests as backdrop and overlooking snowy peaks of Himalayas.

The table top plains besides appearing a miracle of nature are a place for the valley to jointly celebrate festivals, including the anniversary of sage Ved Vyas, with all grandeur. The trek from Budhi to Chialekh is exhausting but exhilarating. Mother nature appears to welcome the tired pilgrims with warmth and into her soothing arms.

A fantastic view of glaciers on Nepal side, as if bending forward to meet river Kali down below, cannot be lost sight of even by an indifferent traveller. Clouds cavorting in the sky are seen to be gamely competing with each other to enjoy the beauty of the Bugyal. After reaching Chialekh, river Kali goes out of sight briefly. The journey to Gunji is easier through curves with limited ups and downs. The trekking does become slippery and difficult in the event of rains which are unpredictable.

About 7 km from Chialekh, the next significant village is Garbyang, also called the sinking village. It witnessed heavy bombardment from the Chinese in the year 1962, evident from unexploded bombs and mortar shells still preserved there. Probably, it was the biggest habitation in Vyas valley. Besides being an important centre of trade and business with Tibet, it had been a significant place for KMY pilgrims since ancient times. A once prosperous village having tastefully constructed houses with ornate woodwork now lies in a dilapidated state. It lies in an ecologically-sensitive zone along the Tethyan Fault. Its ground surface is now seen broken into undulating terraces. This could also be due to erosion of land along the banks of river Kali flowing forcefully at the village base. The yielding ground has taken toll and many houses have been consumed by sinking ground, by as much as 60 feet in a span of 15 years; adjacent houses now appear at different levels.

The inhabitants, a tribe called "Sauka", however, appear neither scared nor worried by the ground sinking beneath their feet. They have moved out to nearby safe grounds and most of the exquisitely-carved wooden panels are found for sale in Nepalese bazaars. In the winter, people move out to live in Dharchula or villages around to escape the snow and bone-chilling weather.

The next halt for the pilgrims is in Gunji village, which has Napalchyu village close by. Their inhabitants called Gunjiyal and Napalchyal respectively, both belong to the Sauka tribe. River Kutti originating from Limpia-dhura, and appearing from Adi Kailas, unites with river Kali between these two villages. Before merging with Kali, the size of Kutti looks bigger with larger volume of water. That is how Kali is seen appearing smaller beyond Gunji village.

Folklore and folk songs are galore, associating places around these villages with the Pandavas. They are stated to have lived here before moving to heaven. Festivals are celebrated in their memory singing their tales with rituals regularly by all seven villages of Vyas valley which include Budhi, Garbyang, Gunji, Napalchyu, Nabi, Ragkong, and Kuti. There are any number of tales and beliefs concerning the Pandavas and usage of flora and fauna by people for different purposes. According to one such belief, on the way to Adi Kailas from Gunji, the Pandavas had lived incognito in Kuti village. In the course of time, this village became famous in the name of Kunti, the mother of Pandavas. It is pronounced as Kuti due to phonetic changes with local influence. Mountain ranges overlooking Kuti are known as Kunti mountains, Pandava mountains, etc. It is also believed that ruins of the Fort of Pandavas still exist in Kuti. Locals associating themselves with the heroes of *Mahabharata* take pride in remembering their glorious heritage.

At Gunji (at 3,200 metres, 10,500 ft.), pilgrims from KMY groups are required to undergo acclimatization for two nights and also to pass their final health check-up by ITBP doctors for continuing the onward journey. Typically, some pilgrims do not pass the health grade, and though hugely disappointed have no option but to return to Dharchula and Delhi along with a batch on its return leg from Kailas-Manasarovar. The risk of high-altitude sickness increases exponentially after the pilgrims leave Gunji to climb up to Lipulekh Pass via Kalapani. Treatment of medical emergency on Chinese side would be prohibitively expensive, besides which access to even Indian Consulate or Embassy over thousands of miles away would be difficult and contact with family in India sporadic at best. Another briefing by ITBP to prepare yatris for bigger challenges ahead is given here.

Pilgrims receive a warm welcome from the villagers. Together with ITBP besides playing cricket and performing folk dances, they regaled us with the rhythms of musical instruments, which also convey a rich local culture and hospitality. A spirited nationalism appears ingrained in the DNA of people residing in remote villages bordering China, abundantly found in their songs, music and gestures. Early next morning, yatris plant saplings at 'Manasarovar Van' at the ITBP camp leaving a positive environmental footprint.

It is said that the Himalayan ecology is a text book case. This becomes increasingly evident when the journey advances from Gunji. Vegetative growth becomes limited to a few plant species. Naked rocks and mountains around the route offer a different experience. Travellers can also take a gentle walk to Nabi, a village 3 km from Gunji. Upon arrival, they are greeted with a traditional welcome and treated to a conglomerate of Kumauni cuisine, folk dance and music. A jot prior to reaching the Kali temple is Sheshnag mountain, as if standing for an audience with Goddess Kali besides standing on guard across the river Kali.

Kalapani, at 3,570 metres (11,000 ft.), is 10 km from Gunji. The trek was far easier even in the year 2015 when I undertook the journey with a good road formation almost up to Kalapani. Now, the Kailas-Manasarovar Road has become motorable right up to Lipulekh Pass. Immediately after crossing river Kali, one finds a beautiful modern temple of Kali in a serene environment. A huge fountain of water appearing from the bottom of a big boulder by the side of the temple is said to be the origin of the river.

Aboriginal people inhabiting Vyas valley observe festivities for a fortnight in the second half of Bhadrapada (भाद्रपद शुक्लपक्ष) every year. The whole period is spent in propitiating deities by offering prayers. Vyas valley looks more like a valley of flowers due to blossoming of a variety of flowers as if mother nature too participates smilingly in these festivities. People in Kuti village celebrate a festival in the memory of Kunti, while every 12 years Gunji celebrates Victory Day for their victory over "Jumla Rule" of Nepal.

As noted earlier, Narayan Swami had played a seminal role in promoting education, sanitation, and drinking water, creating cultural consciousness, removing superstitions and uniting villagers of Chaudas and Vyas valleys. People of Sauka tribe inhabiting these valleys continue to follow the traditions of singing devotional songs in praise of Narayana and reciting his names. Even after generations, the great saint is remembered fondly and respectfully. These festivals are also occasions for them to express their gratitude towards this visionary saint, who was seen as a combination of Bhakti Yoga and Karma Yoga.

According to local lore, sage Vyas composed four Vedas, Brahma sutras, Mahabharata and eighteen Puranas living in a cave (व्यास गुफा) situated in Vyas valley, besides performing deep meditation there without distraction. A mass of rocky mountain facing the temple of Kali from the north-eastern side shows the inaccessible cave of Vyas.

In memory of this greatest ancient sage and father figure of Sanatan Dharma, a temple has been constructed on the grasslands of Chialekh. In Gunji village too, another temple stands constructed dedicated to him. A festival and religious gathering is held every year in the month of August in the memory sage Vyas. Villagers from Vyas valley regularly visit Kalapani to see the cave of Vyas on the mountain rocks in front of the Kali temple in Kalapani. In past, there were deeper trading relationship between villages of Vyas valley and Tibet. Natural wonders in terms of medicinal plants, forests, variety of flowers, waterfalls, rivers, streams, changing ecology, mythology-based tradition, etc. place Vyas valley in a unique position.

Nabhidang, at 4,246 metres (13,930 ft.), at a distance of 8 km from Kalapani is the last destination for night halt before crossing the border at Lipulekh Pass. It is an uphill climb from Kalapani, and the mystical Kali is soon left behind.

Origin of Kali and Lipulekh

Popularly, the fountain of water by the side of Kali temple in said to be the origin of river Kali. The geographical reality and mythological narratives, however, tell another tale about the actual source of this critical river. According to this tale, the actual origin of this river is Lipulekh mountain. In the Manas Khand, the importance of river Kali is established with its origin finding vivid description which fully matches the ground reality as far as source of this river is concerned.

In chapter 116 of Manas Khand, it is said that sage Vyas had once summoned sage Suta, Jaimini and Sukhdev along with others in connection with a Yajna (यज्ञ). Kuber, in the Himalayas, desired to conduct this Yajna successfully. When the sages arrived in the Himalayas honouring the invitation of Kuber to participate in the Yajna, they were taken to Lipi mountain decorated ornamentally with white and bright snow. Here, they found many priceless metals. In the place where the Yajna was to be performed on the right side of the mountain peak, the host Lord Kuber was awaiting them. As soon as the sages arrived, the host stood up in respect to greet them:

दक्षिणे शिखराणां वै आसीने लिपिपर्वते।
तत्र सम्पूजिता सर्वे धनदेवमहात्मना।।

On the western side of the Lipi mountain, sage Vyas was residing in a specially made Ashram for him. His radiating face was energizing and illumining the atmosphere from the divine position created for him. A prayer was made before sage Vyas to invite the holy river from heaven for her sacred water to be used in the Yajna. Accepting the prayers of Kuber, sage Vyas called upon river Mandakini from her home in heaven where she used to be served by sages. The river obliged and came crashing down to the Himalayas with her forceful landfall on the head of Lord Mahakal (Shiva) who was engrossed in deep meditation. The disruption of his samadhi enraged him. The situation was aggravated by the arrogant demeanour of river Mandakini, and Lord Mahakal entangled her in his black matted hair. Finally, on being released from the captivity of his matted hairs after some time, the river became black in her appearance and came to be called 'Shyama' or Kali:

महाकालस्य शिरसि पपात मुनिसेविता
महाकालस्य रोषेण श्यामा मन्दाकिनी ह्यभूत्।।

Nature bountiful and destructive

Vyas valley or a valley full of flowers

Panoramic views enroute from Chialekh to Kalapani

Garbyang, the Sinking Village

Kalapani to Lipulekh Pass for cross-over into Tibet

Two nights at Gunji; Kali temple at Kalapani; Vyas's cave high-up

Sheshnag mountain; Kalapani to Nabhidang; Mount Api

Om Parvat with ॐ naturally engraved

Lipulekh, panoramic views, under a thick layer of snow

Lipulekh Pass-India, when the snow had melted

Lipulekh Pass-Tibet, leeward side

After touching the water of the holy river, Kuber performed *Bajapeya* (बाजपेय) Yajna. Mandakini had arrived in Lipi mountain on the request of sage Vyas. River Sarayu merges with it after covering some distance. According to a mythological description, the holy bath and religious rituals performed at their confluence, bring multiple benefits.

Chapters 117-121 of Manas Khand clearly speak of a holy place called '*Hotri Tirtha*' (होतृतीर्थ) in Shyama or Kali river, with Chaturdransht (चतुर्दंष्ट) mountain (Chaudas) on its right. Yupa tirtha is in the vicinity. The *Krittikas* (कृत्तिका) were blessed to enjoy the company of Kartikeya after they took a holy dip in river Shyama. Another river originating from the Himalayas named Galanti (*Gori*) also meets Kali. Lord Shiva in the form of Hanseshwar adorns the *Hansa tirtha* situated on the snowy mountain between Kali and Gori rivers. One should offer prayers to Lord Hanseshwar situated by the side of river Kali after a holy dip in the river to reserve his place in the Shiva Loka. These chapters contain a number of narratives in relation to holy places in mountains around river Kali though it is difficult to correlate all those places with their present denominations.

In chapter 122 of Manas Khand, the origin of river Gori (Galanti) is said to lie in Panchachuli mountain range. It is stated that after piercing the buttocks of the Himalayas, river Gori which started flowing under directions from Goddess Parvati, meets river Kali. Chapters 123 to 132 provide details of other rivers and streams originating variously in the Himalayas who surrender their existence in Kali river. It requires in-depth and comprehensive research to relate those rivers, streams and places to their current names and differentiate the actual position from what could be mere imaginations.

The trek from Kalapani to Lipulekh is strenuous and difficult. Covering 19 km from Gunji to Nabhidang, the route offers a great exposure to rapid topographical and ecological changes. Kalapani area presents a vibrant form of nature with its expressions in shape of river Kali including its source, other streams, waterfalls, hot water springs, Vyas Gufa in a rocky mountain facing frontally, and a beautiful modern Kali temple. The stretch of 9 km after Kalapani is without vegetative growth barring small shrubs. Nabhidang offers another facet of the same nature which is simply fantastic. The view of the majestic *Om Parvat* with its revealing snow-cover is beyond imagination; simply divine.

The gigantic letter Om (ॐ) is etched deep, proportionately, as though by man, on the mountain peak. Clouds are seen constantly changing their positions as if to embrace the essence of Om in 360 degrees covering it from every direction. They keep appearing in formations presenting picturesque scenes. Om (ॐ) is Brahman or Ultimate Reality according to Indian philosophical texts (ओमित्येकाक्षरं ब्रह्म-भगवद्गीता). The name of the Ultimate Reality naturally appearing at the peak of a mountain seems suggestive of this truth– the nameless, formless and attributeless, who is invisible to the gross senses, has manifested itself in this form, visible from far and wide, by one and all, as the pinnacle of a mountain to boost the confidence of seekers in the Ultimate Reality. That this manifestation is found in the Himalayas enroute to the Holy Mount Kailas which is said to be the centre or core of the entire creation and where the deity is said to reside point to the compelling reality of the spirit and spirituality of the mighty Himalayas, the abode of Gods. It, thus, also follows that we should be equally respectful towards the other gross manifestations of that Ultimate Reality appearing in various form of Nature.

After spending the night at Nabhidang, pilgrims have to rise in the wee hours to climb Mount Lipu through a steep chilly trek over 7 km. More than half the distance of this most difficult trek on the Indian side has to be covered in the dark, in order to meet the rendezvous hour designated at 7:30 a.m. with Chinese immigration and customs authorities at the precipice of Lipulekh Pass. The Himalayas are steep and slippery on the Tibetan side of Lipulekh Pass. It is a surreal experience where nature shows how two sides of the same coin can be so different. The experience of meeting and greeting Chinese immigration authorities standing on a precipice has its quixotic moments. The Indian side of immigration and customs had been cleared at their camp soon after leaving Kalapani the previous day. ITBP in larger numbers than hitherto accompanies the group of pilgrims.

Half of the distance of this extremely difficult trek has to be negotiated on thick layers of snow to reach the pass at Lipulekh at an altitude of 5,335 metres (17,503 ft). The onward journey to Kailas-Manasarovar on the Indian side ends at Lipulekh coinciding with the morning sunrise. It takes nearly four to five hours to trek this last leg, although the return journey being downhill most of the time gets completed in less than three hours. It is difficult to describe the scenic beauty of Lipulekh radiating with the rising sun. Pilgrims find themselves in a surreal world. The shape and size of river Kali which becomes thinner and smaller at Kalapani becomes traceless and soundless here.

Lipulekh Pass has been the gateway of routine trade, commerce, and cultural exchanges between the peoples of India and of Tibet since time immemorial though now the latter are under the control of China. A few kilometres below Lipulekh is Taklakot on the Tibetan side, which also serves as a military garrison town. The town even today continues to be the main centre of trade and business. It is said that the soldiers of Maharaj Gulab Singh, a former ruler of Kashmir, had returned via Taklakot and Lipulekh after their commander-in-chief General Zoravar Singh, famous for his legendary bravery was killed in Purang valley of Tibet. Despite many other access routes, the majority of traders, pilgrims and saints from India preferred to visit Tibet and Kailas-Manasarovar via Lipulekh and Taklakot in the past.

It has been stated earlier that river Kali defines the border between India and Nepal. Kali is known as Mahakali in Nepal. The route leading to the origin of Kali and finally to the significant part of the Trans-Himalayas, namely, Kailas-Manasarovar, despite being difficult is indeed pleasurable. How can one feel tired in the home land of Lord Shiva and his family? It is not for nothing, Gods and Goddesses and sages and seers found the Himalayas including its beautiful valleys and rivers an ideal place to evolve, enjoy and achieve the highest goal of life. When the demons were terrorizing the dwellers of heaven and earth, it was in their shelter of the Himalayas that Sages and Gods prayed for protection. It was here that the Divine Power took the form of Goddess Durga to destroy the demons.

5

Pilgrim Touch-Points in Tibet

After trekking continuously for four days (excluding acclimatization period of one day and two nights at Gunji) through an ever-changing and ebullient terrain that combined sensual beauty and physical pain, crossing Mount Lipu/ Lipi and heading towards Taklakot disorients you as though you are now on a different planet with mile-after-mile of stillness and calm in its elevated vastness.

One also realises soon enough the difference built-in freedoms in the pilgrimage and ready spontaneity of the local populace and children on the Indian side can make. They add an incredible zing to your experiences and help you grapple with and overcome the surprises and risks of a young and super-active terrain at every bend and turn. In sharp and egregious contrast, the regimented officialdom with militarism frontally visible creates hesitation and fear at every nook and corner. It erodes and undermines the warmth and cultural ties going back for millennia, as though before time itself began, on the magical colours of the earthy flat landscapes and ease of traversing through the superb road infrastructure on the Tibetan plateau.

After virtually slip-sliding down the snowy terrain (it was early June) for the first 5-6 km immediately after the cross-over at Lipulekh Pass, it suddenly becomes quite comfortable travelling in luxury buses arranged by the local administration to reach Taklakot another 13 km away in no more than twenty minutes. The aerial distance is unlikely to be more than 5 km.

Taklakot

The city centre Taklakot, situated in Purang valley of Tibet, is at an altitude of 3,940 metres (12,930 ft.). It is a prosperous town equipped with various modern amenities, big buildings, and urban infrastructure, including good hotels. It is the main business centre in the valley besides being a tri-junction point of Tibet/China, India and Nepal replete with a Chinese military garrison and cantonment just across the Karnali river northeast from the ruined fort and monasteries of Burang, the ancient trading post. The presence of small traders and businessmen of the neighbouring places of these countries can be marked here. Nepalese workforce is found in good numbers. Indian and Nepalese currencies are accepted for the day-to-day business transactions, informally, without much hesitation. Personnel of the Chinese Army are seen roaming around frequently. Indigenous Tibetans in the city appear to be completely marginalized. Business and institutional establishments are dominated by people from mainland China with negligible presence of indigenous community.

A great deal of transformation seems to have taken place in Taklakot in the last few years. From the wide roads with paved side-walks, big official buildings set up cheek-by-jowl with hotels and pilgrimage and tourist paraphernalia, and other infrastructures, it is impossible to guess the abject poverty, extreme backwardness, and lack of physical infrastructure in the hinterland of Tibet. Life in Taklakot is controlled and it is not possible to move around freely or spontaneously and mix with inhabitants. The old Tibetan villages including their traditional monasteries around Taklakot are found virtually abandoned.

Thus, in sharp contrast with the modern well-developed town, a walk through the old town on the other side of the river revealed broken small hutments, curiously padlocked with new shining locks on dilapidated doors. A once thriving market-place for indigenous handicraft and traded-items was simply a ghost town. The only person seen singing rather musically through this desolation was an old skeleton of a half-mad fakir. After taking some packed sandwiches from us which we happened to be carrying, he wandered off as quickly as he emerged on the bridge separating the two halves of the town. The visit to Shepeling Gompa was tricky but quite a treat.

The smiling indigenous people, shying away as soon as the military presence was felt in close vicinity, informed that the large ancient fort of Tegla Kar (Lying Tiger Fort) seen quite intriguingly on a cliff above the town and the Simbiling Monastery were both totally destroyed in 1967 by the Chinese during the Cultural Revolution. Whatever was left of the fort is not accessible to pilgrims due to the location of the garrison of the People's Liberation Army of China at its base. In fact, pilgrims are expected to remain detached from locals, circumspect and vigilant to avoid being misunderstood, which could lead to unpleasantness beyond the simple admonishment.

Tsegu Gompa (Nine-Storey Monastery) partially restored by Buddhist Lamas 4 decades later is a delight to visit by reaching its terraces through a series of ladders. Said to be the place where *Sudhana* a previous incarnation of the Buddha lived, or by some a Bon establishment.

The town centre of Taklakot is situated in the Karnali valley of Purang county. Though natural vegetative growth in Tibetan plateau is largely missing, some carefully organized, cultivated plantations alongside the black-topped roads that cut through the undulations of topography have been raised in and around Taklakot town. The canal drawn from the Karnali river flowing by the side of Taklakot has also helped in promoting settled agriculture in some villages of Purang valley. Greenery in the agricultural lands and flowering crops are suggestive of subsistence agriculture.

On the right bank of river Karnali, presence of Tibetan Buddhist monks become visible in Gompas created by cutting through rocks. Indeed, in the villages of Purang valley, the life-style including clothes used by local youth indicate the effect of modernity in the highly tradition-bound superstitious Tibetan society. Official rudeness experienced in Taklakot town is not felt in equal measure after moving away from the town. In villages around Taklakot town, local community is found involved in agricultural activities and in day to day chores. Places around Taklakot are also witnessing physical transformation rather rapidly.

The remaining stretch of Kailas-Manasarovar Yatra excluding the circumambulation of Mount Kailas is completed by luxury buses. The sense of identification, belongingness and warm hospitality that comes spontaneously and constantly en-route in the Indian side, however, is missing in Taklakot and occasionally found in the subsequent leg of pilgrimage despite the higher degree of physical comforts on offer. Some arrogance with rudeness from the official guides and local people is not uncommon. Chinese military establishment had a sizeable presence all the way to Darchen, the next night halt.

Toyo and the memorial of General Zoravar Singh

Toyo village at a distance of 06 km from Taklakot is one of

the most prosperous villages of Purang valley. It also occupies a significant place in local history because the Dogra General Zoravar Singh, of the then Maharaja Gulab Singh of Kashmir, having established control over a large part of Tibet in 1841, suffered sudden defeat in this village. Having entered into Tibet from Leh with 1,500 soldiers, he had taken effective control over the forts and monasteries on his way after defeating the local warriors and had established his headquarters in *Tirthpuri* (तीर्थ पुरी).

The brave General defeated the strong Tibetan army of 10,000 soldiers in a place near Barakha/Parakha before marching towards Taklakot. He left the majority of his soldiers behind along with his deputy, Captain Basti Ram and proceeded to Gartok with handful of his warriors to drop his wife there. On the way back, he faced an unexpected assault in Toyo from the large Tibetan army who were duly assisted by the Chinese. Despite limited resources, he fought against the enemy forces with valour. Tibetan soldiers were scared of the General and believed that divine forces under some tantric influence were operating in him for which ordinary bullets could not pierce his body. Therefore, golden bullets were used to kill him. His body was cut into pieces after he was killed in the battle.

After the martyrdom of General Zoravar Singh, his last rites were performed with full honour. A memorial was constructed in his memory. Some organs of his body including private parts were kept in Simbiling Gompa. It is said that one arm of this great warrior has been preserved in nearby Sakya Gompa. In many other Gompas, his vestments, arms, trophies of victories, etc. have been kept. Perhaps, it is the only and unique example in the world history of wars that a defeated army General is remembered with so much of respect and a memorial is established by the victor army in his honour. This memorial was destroyed by the Chinese during their cultural revolution. In the last leg of Kailas-Manasarovar journey, pilgrims are afforded an opportunity to visit Toyo village to pay their respects to the General at the remnants of destroyed memorial/ *Samadhi* (समाधि), on their pilgrimage's return leg.

Khojarnath

The famous Gompa of Khojarnath is located 18 km from Taklakot on river Karnali. It is one of the most beautiful ancient monuments in Purang county, and visited by people from all parts of Tibet round the year. Frequented by Indians routinely in the past, according to Hindu tradition and belief, this Gompa is known as *Khechar Tirtha* (खेचर तीर्थ).

Born in the second half of tenth century (980 or 982 AD) in a village near what is Dhaka today, the Buddhist philosopher Dipankar Shrigyan arrived here in the year 1034, and spent the entire rainy season here. Swami Pranavanand in his master-piece of research, Kailas-Manasarovar, has cited an interesting tale in relation to this famous Gompa described as Khochar/ Karchhak which is as follows:

> *"Seven Acharyas from India once took seven loads of silver to Kardung and deposited it with Jambyang Thakpa, the then King of the place and went away saying that they would return in seven years. But they did not turn up even after nine years. So the King gave the silver to two silver-smiths, one a Nepali by name Ashadharma and the other a Mohammadan by name Vankulla and ordered them to make a divine idol out of it. Accordingly, the smiths melted the whole silver to mould it into an idol but suddenly there sprang a big image of Jambyang out of it on its own accord (Svayambhu) out of the molten silver.*

A Lama and his disciple were staying on the sandy banks of Karnali where the present Khochar Gompa stands. Every night the disciple used to see a light on the sand when he would go to fetch water though he would see nothing in the daytime there. One day the Lama asked his disciple to pile up a heap of stones at the place where he saw the light, and the disciple did accordingly. To his great surprise, the heap of stones became a big boulder by next morning. The Lama said that the light was the spirit of Jambyang.

Having heard of Svayambhu (self-formed) idol of Jambyang, the King of Kardung ordered that the idol should be brought to Kardung to be installed in a temple. Accordingly, the image was put in a two-horse carriage and was being taken towards Kardung. The Spirit of Jambyan entered the idol and it was stuck up on the boulder, and said 'Khor-chhak – I have come here and will stay here only'. This is the first utterance of the idol.

Then a Gompa was constructed for the image by the King. When the King was thinking of getting a pedestal made for the idol, it spoke out a second time, 'Let nobody- man, beast, bird, or insect- enter the Gompa for seven days. Accordingly, the monastery gates were closed; but on the fifth day, the Konyer (keeper of idol), in his anxiety to see if the lamps inside were burning or not, opened the doors. He saw the divine smiths that were working out the pedestal or Simhasana, had entered the image and the pedestal was left incomplete. Later on, Vishvakarma, the divine architect, made the silver idols of Chhagna-dorje and Chenresig.

The idol spoke for a third time, 'If the Map chhu rises, it comes near the monastery and I will be taken away by the waters; so, keep the image of Jechun Doma (Tara) facing the river. If anybody makes an embankment his sins of 500 lives shall be washed away; if any one feeds the workmen, sins of 10 lives shall be washed away; and if one puts, even a small stone as big as a thumb, on the embankment with pure heart, the sins of one life will be washed away'.

Once some soldiers entered the Gompa and stabbed the thigh of the idol wherefrom milk came out. The idol spoke a fourth time, 'Oh great sinner!' whereupon all the soldiers went out of the temple, but the one who had actually stabbed the idol died in the temple gate by vomiting blood.

The King of southern region had two Queens but no sons. They did all sorts of Pujas but in vain. The image spoke for the fifth time, 'Come here, Queens, do three prostration-salutes to me, you will have three sons. The Queens did so and later, they had three sons.

One great Lama by name Chang-nyun came here, when, the image spoke out for the sixth time, 'Remove the paper-bird from my back which has been placed by some Ngagpa (black magician). A Ngagpa usually draws the picture of a bird and some other formula on a paper and performs some incantations and rites and puts it in the wall of a house. After a period of 7, 9, or 21 years depending upon the strength of incantations, the bird comes to life and flies away and the person or idol concerned breaks to pieces. Such an incantation paper was kept behind the idol of Jambyang. The Lama Chang-nyum took out the paper-bird which was just fluttering and threw it in fire with tongs.

When Kyangun-Zingba-Nurbu, the Lama who has constructed the existing Gossul Gompa, went to Khochar, the idol of Jambyang spoke for the seventh time, 'The flower in my hand has been taken away by a soldier. It will be good if you can replace it'. The gold-silver flower studded with cat's eye (Vaidurya) in the middle, was replaced by the Lama. The gold lamp in front of the image was presented to the Gompa by the same Lama. It is believed by Tibetans that the image of Jambyang would speak out six times more after which the world would see the day of resurrection".

It would be of interest to share here that a similar mythical story exists in relation to the making of idol of Lord Jagannath in Puri. According to this popular tale, the King of Malava Indra Dyumna once heard about the existence of Nila Madhava (नील-माधव) in blood and flesh in the Neelachal of Puri and quietly came with his family for an audience of the Lord of the Universe. But, by the time the King reached the specific place, other Gods from heaven had already landed there and lifted Nila Madhava to heaven. Seeing the boundless faith of the King who was still awaiting an audience with Nila Madhava in Puri, one day a divine voice from the sky was heard by him that Lord Nila Madhava or Jagannath in the form of a "wooden body" (दारु ब्रह्म) would definitely present himself to the devotee King of Malava.

After living at Nilachal for some time one day the King saw a big piece of wood floating in the sea towards its shore. The King decided to get the idol of Lord Nila Madhava made from that piece of wood. At this juncture, a master sculptor named Bishashrava suddenly appeared before the King. He agreed to prepare the idol of Nila Madhava on the condition that none would distract him in his work inside a closed room and that he himself would come out to inform when the idol gets ready. The King gracefully accepted, and accordingly, Bishashrava undertook the task. Even after many days inside the closed room when there was no information from the sculptor, the Queen of Indra Dyumna got worried as Bishashrava had remained inside without food and water. Thinking that his health might have suffered, she opened the door to find half-made idols of Jagannath, Balabhadra and Subhadra. Bishashrava was missing without any trace in the room. The Queen repented and cried in pain for what she had done. In the meanwhile, a voice from the sky directed that those half-made idols should be put in the temple. The idols of Lord Jagannath, Subhadra and Balabhadra remain in the same form till date.

It may be of relevance to note that Puri happened to be an important centre of Buddhism in the distant past. It is not rare to find similarities between the mythological tales of Hinduism and Buddhism. There are many places considered to be equally holy in the ancient Hindu and Buddhist literature, Kailas and Manasarovar included.

Revered Swami Pranavanand in his book *ibid* has given another fascinating account of Khojarnath Gompa which might interest the readers:

> *"In the duvang or image hall there are three beautiful images of three of the most important Bodhisattvas made of silver standing on an artistically designed pedestal or a bracket about 5 feet high. The images are placed on big lotuses. The Simhasana, including lotuses, are made of Ashta-dhatus or eight metals. The middle image Jambyang (Manjughosha) is about 8 feet high and its face is yellow. On its right is the idol of Chenresig (Avalokiteshvara) 7 feet high and its face is white; and on the left is that of Chhagnadorje (Vajrapani) 7 feet high and its face is of blue complexion.*
>
> *These three images are erroneously described as and believed by many credulous people to be those of Rama, Lakshaman, and Sita. It is interesting to note that all three images are of male deities! On either side of these images are twelve images, each about five feet in height, kept in almirahs, six on either side. Of these, eight are the images of Neve-se-gye, three are the duplicates of Khochar images, and one of Khasarpani.*
>
> *The images and pedestals are of South Indian pattern, prepared by Nepalese sculptors. In 1899 a big fire broke out*

in Khojarnath Gompa and destroyed the two side-images-Avalokiteshvara and Vajrapani. Later they were prepared by Tibetan and Nepalese sculptures. Another tradition says that all three images along with pedestal were brought to the monastery from Lanka or Ceylon.

There are several cups of water and butter-lamps made of gold and silver and are artistically arranged in front of the images. There are two big and fierce-looking images each about 8 feet high at the entrance gate of the monastery. The image on the left-hand side is that of Tamdin, the fierce form of Avalokiteshvara and that on the right is of Chhagdar, the fierce form of Amitabh Buddha. Just after entering the duvang, there are four images of the guardian deities of the four quarters six feet high, two on each side. On either side of the image hall are the shelves containing the volumes of Kanjur, kept in perfect order. There are 30 Dabas and a Tulku Lama in this monastery. By the side of the main Gompa there is a mani-khang, a house in which is installed a huge mani-cylinder.

There is big hall in the second building of the monastery where mystic dances called Namdong and annual feasts are held. In the hall is hung a stuffed wild yak and an Indian tiger on one side. There are also the images of Chaba (Maitreya, the coming Buddha), Mahakal and Mahakali, Sange-Pavo-Rapdun, and Yum-Chhamo-Chhok-Chhu-Sange, placed in different rooms. There is big mani-cylinder 10 feet high and 5 feet in diameter.

The sitting image of Maitreya is about 22 feet in height. Due to its gigantic appearance, Indian pilgrims wrongly identify it with that of Bhimasen of Mahabharata fame. Sange-Pavo-Rapdun (Buddha-hero-seven) are the images of the seven Buddhas sitting in different mudras (postures)- Gautama Buddha, Maitreya Buddha, Kashyap Buddha, Amitabh

Buddha and others. Ignorant Hindu pilgrims think them to be those of Sapta Rishis- Agastya and others. Yum-Chemo-Chhok-Chhu-Sange (Mother-great-directions-ten-sages) are eleven images sitting in different postures. The middle one is that of the great mother Devi Prajnaparamita and the five images on either side are those of ten quarters (four quarters, four corners, sky and nether land), but not of the eleven Rudras as is erroneously believed by Hindu pilgrims.

There are fine frescos in this image hall, some of which are getting damaged due to rain-water leaking inside. The room is very dark and so, very few visitors are aware of these valuable paintings. A great service would be done to the cause of art if any visitor could take a series of these paintings under flash-light. In the upper storey of the building there is the image hall of Jechun Dome (White Tara) in which there are the volumes of Kanjur. The 21 Avatars of Devi are depicted on the walls of the hall. Adjacent to this hall is the Tanjore Library Hall.

On the back of the Gompa, situated in the midst of mani-walls on the banks of the Karnali, is the gaddi of the great Lachva (translator) Rinchhen-Zangbo, where he delivered sermons for twelve years. There are several houses and donkhangs (Tibetan dharmshalas) very near the Gompa; and the village itself is a little away from it. Khochar is warmer than Taklakot, though more windy. A little down the monastery there is a bridge on the Karnali, crossing which, Nepal territory begins. About a mile from Khochar is Shar, the last village in the Purang valley where pema trees, soft stunted deodars, grow".

Tirtha Puri

People in the good old days undertaking pilgrimage of Kailas-Manasarovar visited Tirtha Puri too. In the Tibetan language and trade-related terminology, Tirtha Puri is known as Tatapuri. It remains an important place and indeed, pilgrims who opt for the route via Kathmandu as I did once, are afforded an opportunity to see this place. It is not on the itinerary of the Yatra organized via Lipulekh by the Government of India. Tirtha Puri is situated in the south-west at a distance of 66 km from Manasarovar. It is closer to the source of river Shatadru (Sutlej) on its left side. The distance is 46 km from Darchen on the western side. People from various parts of Tibet frequent the famous Gompa of Tirtha Puri, and ritually circumambulate it. From Taklakot one could reach Darchen after visiting Tirtha Puri on the same day by road in a motor vehicle.

There are a number of natural hot water springs with varying temperatures in and around Tirtha Puri. The calcium carbohydrate and sulphur emitted by these springs can be seen all over. As the upper layer of sulphur keeps the hot water concealed, fountains of such water are found appearing elsewhere in the vicinity. Sulphur around these fountains looks like ashes. People from far and wide come to bathe in these hot waters, which according to popular belief, is a natural cure for gastric and dermatological ailments, besides backache, arthritis, etc.

According to a mythological story, Bhasmasur (भस्मासुर) the demon king, had performed serious penance in Tirtha Puri by the side of a hot water spring to propitiate Lord Shiva, who himself was in the state of deep meditation in Mount Kailas. When Lord Shiva was pleased and blessed the demon king with powers to fulfil his wishes, he tried to exercise such powers to over-power and make captive the beautiful Goddess Parvati. As a result of his misadventure and temerity, he had to pay the price by burning himself. It is said that the huge body of the demon got converted into the heap of ashes. Hindu pilgrims carry these earthen ashes, considering them to be pure and beneficial.

Yellow earth found while traversing through Tirtha Puri is also carried by some pilgrims attaching purity and holiness to it, to put it on their forehead. Tibetan pilgrims bow their heads and embrace the stones near the monastery to express their respectful conviction. General Zoravar Singh had made Tirtha Puri his headquarter during his victory march over Tibet. Just after one hundred years in 1941, some Mohammadan robbers invaded the monastery of Tirtha Puri and burnt the Buddhist literature in manuscripts preserved in the famous Gompa of Tirtha Puri. They went back after also robbing the locals of their wealth and other valuables.

Tibetan Plateau and Pilgrimage to the Sacred Lake

Shepeling Gompa in a ridge of caves high above Taklakot

Samadhi of General Zoravar Singh

Khechar Tirtha (खेचर तीर्थ); *Duvang Hall of Khojarnath Gompa*

Gurla-Mandhata with the two mighty Lakes

Gurla-Mandhata seen in elevation; Smiling down its south-view on Manasarovar and Rakshastal (source: C.J. Wang)

Looking up North, Rakshastal and Manasarovar – two mighty lakes, separated after birth?
Source: Satellite image found without accreditation

Gurla-Mandhata, tall and distinctive

Rakshastal-Mandhata; Manasarovar-Mandhata; breath-taking

King Gurla-Mandhata, lording over Barka Plains

Sacred Manasarovar, no words can do justice

Divine Manasarovar with Kailas; Sacred lake is oceanic in ambit

Manasarovar: Winter freeze; Source: **Unknown.**

6

Gurla-Mandhata Mountain Range

To the far east of Lipulekh travelling through flat terrain mired in earthy brown and rust soils and rocks with streaks of red and green, the silver-white Gurla-Mandhata mountain range can not fail to strike the attention of pilgrims. Standing at 7,694 metres (25,243 ft.), the Gurla-Mandhata could be scaled successfully via its north side only in 1985. This Nalankar Himal sub-range is also called Naimona'nyi in Tibetan language, meaning "*mountains of heaped up slabs of black herbal medicines*" and are the source of many streams emptying in the holy Manasarovar, which is thus replete with nutrient-rich water sourced in the snows of Gurla-Mandhata. Pilgrims enjoy the beauty of these streams in a pleasant and comfortable journey on this part of the Tibetan plateau, albeit filled with high anticipation of rapidly reaching Rakshastal, Manasarovar, and Mount Kailas.

Moving forward towards Mount Kailas, when it first comes into sight Rakshastal looks like a huge blue water-body or mini ocean surrounded by a frozen desert. This wonder of nature on the roof of the Earth, with its vastness extending as far as the naked eye can see, appears as if it is a mirror image of the clear blue sky within touching distance above. The lake is fed by numerous streams with their source in Mount Kailas to the north.

The sparkling snow-capped lofty Mount Kailas, the abode of Lord Shiva, is situated very close to this water body. Even on a sunny day clouds in their various benign shapes and aggressive postures are seen to seek to embrace an unrelenting holy mountain only to disappear in wisps. This unique lake brings thoughts of relief and joy to the water-parched banks and wider environs where not a stalk of grass is seen to be growing.

From the shores of Rakshastal, the exuberating sight of the silver-white, massive, dome-shaped Mount Kailas, curiously surrounded by naked mountains, looks like a temple artistically decorated and fit for serving the abode of the Ultimate Reality. The all-seeing eyes, and appearance of a central pathway, and protective crowning hood of the serpent, beckon you meditatively and make your journey to Shangri-La quite complete. The view in a sunny day is simply incredible.

After covering a distance of another about 6 miles pilgrims reach the most phenomenal and intriguing lake of Manasarovar. Fed by streams that flow down from Gurla-Mandhata, a naturally-created canal of about 6-mile length serves as an outlet for release of the surplus water of Manasarovar in the Rakshastal. Unlike Rakshastal, Manasarovar despite being deeper and much bigger in size is seen to have many moods and shades when seen from various angles, vantage points, and in different time zones during sunny days and moonlit nights. The beauty of this lake is simply beyond the reach of words.

Perhaps, it is for this reason Manasarovar is said to have been created by the supreme architect of the universe, Brahma, through his divine will for the benefit and use of supernatural beings. Mount Kailas in the north and Mandhata mountains in the east overlook the lake in which sages and seers, Gods and Goddesses descending from heaven are said to come for their holy dip every morning at Brahma muhurta. The images of mountains in the north and east reflected on the shimmering and glistening lake waters contribute to its changing colours and effervescence throughout the day that makes its beauty truly impossible to be captured. The Lake evokes feelings which are spiritual, sensory, and phenomenological at the same time, and thus must be experienced with all respective faculties and senses operating at their most heightened state of consciousness.

Hindu mythology describes Mandhata as the first king on Earth after its creation. The mountain is named after this king considered to be the greatest of all times. More on this later. In the tenth chapter of *Manas Khand*, *Skanda Purana*, there is an interesting episode to explain the heroism of the great ruler Mandhata that resulted in creation or discovery of Manasarovar. The story goes like this:

Born in the clan of *Vaivasvat Manu*, Mandhata who desired to create a name for himself in the history, fell in love with the Earth which had taken form of a beautiful youthful woman. Indeed, this lady had herself appeared before him at midnight to convey her determination to marry him. She wanted the king to satisfy her physical hunger as she had fallen deeply in love with him. She vowed to live and die with him and face every situation without ever raising any complaint through out their life spent in togetherness. When the lady perceived that King Mandhata was lukewarm to her desires and overtures, she tried to intimidate him stating than no king had ever been able to transform her to old age from her ever-lasting youthfulness. That is why she deserted them one-by-one. She had now decided to be in lifelong companionship of the legendary King Mandhata.

Even after being told by Mandhata that no one on Earth can remain in the same youthful form forever and that she would have to swear by Lord Shiva's feet to be truthful to her words, the Earth-incarnate lady promised that she would remain his partner if the King succeeds in her aging by marrying her. After the lady vows to remain truthful to her promise, King Mandhata married her. They started enjoying life together exploring the Universe.

With the passage of time, King Mandhata decided to conduct a *Rajsuya Yajna* (राजसूय यज्ञ) and told the Earth in the form of his beautiful youthful wife to remain by his side. He also shared with her his decision of going deep into the forest for meditation as he was approaching the third phase of his life called *Vanaprasth* (वानप्रस्थ). In accordance with the principles of *Dharma* that had been followed by predecessors in his clan, King Mandhata needed to enter *Vanaprastha* which called for leading a detached life in solitude and for pursuing meditative practices. Rajarshi Mandhata explained to his wife that after leading *Vanaprastha* life, he would be eligible to have access to heaven with her and together they would then enjoy heavenly comforts and happiness.

Upon hearing the decision of Mandhata to enter *Vanaprastha*, Earth-incarnate laughingly asserted, '*O Rajarshi! I am still in my youth. I cannot go to heaven while still performing my functions as a wife. If you have become physically weak and old, why do you want me too to be weak and grow old to acquire eligibility for access to heaven*?'

This response enraged King Mandhata. With unbound anger, he drew out his sword from its scabbard and was ready to attack the earth-incarnate, still as youthful and beautiful as when she had first proposed marriage with him. She ran away fearing that the King seething in anger was going to destroy her with his fearsome sword. But when she saw the

King giving her chase, she entered and sought refuge in the house of the Himalayas. When she found that Mandhata had followed her unchecked into the house, she moved out and reached the Manas region created by Brahma's divine desire. King Mandhata reached there too and struck on her head with his sword. The youthful lady again entered the Himalayas and vanished deep into the last layers of the earth or Patal. Seeing her assimilating with the deepest layers of earth, Mandhata started digging the whole Manas region even though it was highly respected by Gods. After digging deep for a long time using the corner of his bow, the King could not discover his spouse.

Ultimately, Mandhata found the sovereign symbol of Lord Shiva in the form of a royal golden swan. He went into a trance instantly after seeing the golden swan. Rivers started originating from the places he had dug up. Seeing the Manas region created by Brahma in some disarray, Rajarshi Mandhata created a huge oceanic space 200 yojanas in length, 60 yojanas in width and 10 yojanas in depth. This space got filled up by the waters flowing from the rivers originating from the areas dug up by the King using the pressure of his bow:

वैवस्वतकुले जातो मान्धाता नाम भूपतिः।
तेनायं खनितो विप्रा महता कारणेन च।।
प्रकाशितोऽयं तेनेव नदीभिश्चापि ह्यन्वितः।।

King Mandhata offered prayers with flowers before the sovereign symbol (shivalinga) that had appeared in the form of a golden swan. Witnessing this event, all the Gods showered respect on him while singing songs in his admiration. After this event, an aircraft from heaven suddenly appeared and took off carrying King Mandhata to the kingdom of Lord Vishnu (विष्णु लोक). The wishes of Mandhata were thus fulfilled instantly. Sages and seers admired the King who had held public service supreme in his mind and actions, and who had brought to light the phallus of Lord Shiva in the Manas region created by none other than Brahma himself.

According to another episode narrated in the seventh chapter of *Manas Khand*, seeing the arrival of the great Maharshi Dattatreya, King of all mountains, the Himalayas propitiated him by offering all services and prayers most respectfully. When he desired to know the reason for his sudden arrival, the Great Sage Dattatreya said that despite all mountains, including the Vindhyas, having all the prerequisites to be counted as holy places, they are hardly comparable with the Himalayas. Elaborating on the greatness and holiness of the Himalayas, Maharshi Dattatreya added that this region was the place where the phallus of Lord Shiva had fallen. Therefore, he was greatly curious to come to this place to experience absolute happiness and satisfaction. He was eager to see it and could not delay coming to the Himalayas which had numerous holy places, including the holy place of *Vaibhava*. On the insistence of the Maharshi Dattatreya, the king of mountains showed him Manasarovar, the divine creation of Brahma. Around the lake were inhabiting sages in caves, enjoying deep meditation and in trance. Dattatreya was thus shown the phallus of Lord Shiva in the form of a royal swan in the centre of Lake Manasarovar.

Maharshi Dattatreya circumambulated Mount Kailas and thereafter proceeded to Kailas, where he met Lord Shiva. Extremely pleased with the devotion and respect showered by him, Lord Shiva wanted Dattatreya to seek wish fulfilment. In response, Dattatreya desired to know as to which was the greatest and holiest mountain on Earth. Lord Shiva responded by saying that although He also resided in the Vindhya Mountains, he had never left the holy land of the Himalayas. All Gods bow before him in the Himalayas all the time.

There is yet another episode in the eighth and ninth chapters of *Manas Khand* containing the experiences of Dattatreya in the Himalayas. After returning, Dattatreya explained the great importance of Mount Kailas to Kashiraj Dhanvantari. He underlined that Manasarovar which was constantly served by swans was created by none other than Brahma through his divine wish, and that Lord Shiva himself graced the holy Lake in the form of a Golden Swan. It may be mentioned here that the most evolved sages who have realized the Ultimate Reality are also called Swans in the ancient metaphysical texts.

तथेत्युक्त्वा च भगवान् ब्रह्मा लोकपितामहः।
मनसा मानसं क्षेत्रं ससर्ज नृपसत्तम।।

लिंगं तन्मध्यगं राजन्स्वर्णहंसमयं शुभम्।
चकार च स्वयं ब्रह्मा मनसा हंससेवितम्।।

Dattatreya further explained to Kashiraj Dhanvantari that there was no place holier and better than Manas region in the Himalayas. This place is origin of many rivers. It is the place where the taste of a few drops of water from the divine lake of Manasarovar guarantees a place in *Shiva Loka* (शिव लोक). One gets liberated from the sins committed and accumulated over hundreds of lives just by touching the droplets of water from Manasarovar. Demitting body in the Manas region also ensures a place in *Brahma Lok* (ब्रह्म लोक). A dip in Manasarovar is as beneficial as the holy bath in the river Ganga. Indeed, the importance of Manas region is beyond the expressive powers of words, concludes Dattatreya.

The aforesaid episodic references of the Himalaya are related to Manas region as a whole, which include Gurla-Mandhata mountain ranges in the greater Himalayas. Needless to say, that Kailas-Manasarovar is the core of this region. The rivers that originated and filled up the water body of

Manasarovar after King Mandhata dug up the place following the Earth-incarnate youthful lady who had become his spouse but had escaped when he entered the third stage or *Vanaprastha* of his life, are known by the present names of Brahmaputra, Karnali, Indus and Sutlej.

7

Manasarovar

Among the forests and mountain *Tirthas* in the Indian subcontinent, which have for long attracted great souls desirous of pursuing their meditative practices in a spiritually-charged atmosphere, the Himalayas have provided the sought-after remoteness from the hustle and bustle of inhabitations, absence of ready accessibility through road and telecom networks, and freedom from worldly distractions. These holy places were considered most conducive to lead a spiritual life. In fact, only the rarest of the rare committed to this most austere life and had the courage and conviction to come to such places to work for self-realization or liberation from the cycle of birth and death. Naturally, Kailas-Manasarovar, abode of the most powerful yet completely detached among Gods, situated in the most inhospitable region of greater Himalayas, attracted only the dedicated ones who were determined to achieve their goal.

Chapter 9 in *Manas Khand* contains an interesting episode in relation to the creation of Manasarovar. When the divine sons of Lord Brahma including sage *Marichi* (मरीचि) came to know that Lord Shiva along with consort Parvati was enjoying the peace and serenity of Mount Kailas and that the place was populated by a number of divine creatures, they decided to proceed to the Himalayas. They found many sages residing there and engaged in meditative practices in this great mountain decorated with silvery snow particles. Soon after, they too started serious penance and got into deep meditation. In this state, they met Parvati and Shiva in the form of a pair of swans, and spent twelve years in meditation in Mount Kailas region. With the arrival of *Hemant Ritu* (हेमन्त ऋतु) preceding winter, when their bodies started wilting without any water in their immediate vicinity, they found themselves too listless, almost without energy to go to river Mandakini. They decided to leave the place for *Brahma Loka* (ब्रह्म लोक) and bring the situation to the notice of the presiding master of his kingdom, Lord Brahma. Acting upon their plan when they pleased Brahma through devotional prayers in his admiration who sought to know the reason for their arrival, the sages submitted their woes in the valley of Mount Kailas at the onset of winter due to distant waters of river Mandakini. The sages pleaded for their woes to be addressed by Brahma, their divine father.

Brahma melted after hearing the plight of his divine sons and created the Manas region using his divine powers to do so. At the centre of the Manas region, Lord Shiva graciously established himself taking the form of a golden swan and thereby enhanced beauty of the place. The river Mandakini or the Ganga came out of her place in heaven where she was relaxing at the feet of Lord Vishnu, and filled up the spaces between Mount Kailas and Mount Gauri with her flowing holy water. In the process, Manasarovar was created and got reputed for being the source of many rivers. The sages left Brahma Loka for their respective *Ashrama* to pursue their meditative practices. They saw the holy Lake Manasarovar and offered prayers before Lord Shiva who had graced its central space in the form of a golden swan.

The earliest narratives about the creation of Manasarovar is found in the epic *Ramayana* written by the sage poet Valmiki, also known to be the first poet to compose in classical Sanskrit. In the twenty fourth canto of *Bal Khand* of the book, sage Vishvamitra is found telling Lord Rama that this water body by the side of Mount Kailas came to be known as Manasarovar as it was created by Brahma exercising his divine powers:

कैलासशिखरे राम मनसा निर्मितं सरः।
ब्रह्मणा नरशार्दूल तेनेदं मानसं सरः।।

In the epic *Mahabharata*, an interesting tale related to the Pandavas involves Mount Kailas. Draupadi, the spouse of five Pandavas once desired to have the flower of golden lotus, emitting the most pleasing odour, from a place called *Vadarikashrama* (वदरीकाश्रम). Her beloved husband Bhimasena left in search for it to fulfil her desire. He reached the natural lake situated near Mount Kailas by the side of Kuber's mansion. In Chapter 153 of *Vana Parva* of *Mahabharata* it is stated that the lake was filled with sweet streams containing nectar originating from the mountains. Water of this lake satiated the thirst of Bhimasena. This lake seems to be none other than Manasarovar:

कैलासशिखराभ्यासे ददर्श शुभकाननाम्
कुबेरभवनाभ्यासे जातां पर्वतनिर्झरे।।

तत्रामृतं रसं शीतं लघुकुन्तीसुतः स्वयम्।
ददर्श विमले तोयं पिबंश्च बहु पाण्डवः।।

In the old mythological texts and other books of the ancient literature, narratives about the existence of a beautiful big lake near Kuber's mansion are found repeatedly. It is mentioned in Chapter 26 of *Kedar Mahatmya* (केदार माहात्म्य) that swan couples used to enjoy and walk happily in Lake Manasarovar. According to this narrative, Kuber used to come to the lake with his spouses to bathe in addition to walking around and taking rest under the banyan tree above its waterline:

हंसयोर्दम्पती पूर्वं मानसाख्ये सरोवरे।
स्थितौ परस्परं प्रेम्णा विहरन्तौ निरन्तरम्।।

कुबेरस्तत्र वै नित्यं विहर्तुं याति साबलः।
चिरं विहृत्य सस्नाय वटमूले समाश्रयत्।।

Due to geographical changes that might have taken place in course of time, there are no trees or flowers in the Kailas-Manasarovar and environs. Another aspect to be taken into account is that stories and parables in Vedic literature and mythological texts convey deeper meanings of the subject matter. Usage of attractive, often hyperbolic imagery, helps in generating interest of common people in serious subjects and are not to be read literally.

Moreover, what is seen by our gross eyes or perceived by other gross senses cannot be portrayed as the only evidence of the Reality. What is non-obvious is far more than what appears obvious to us. It is possible that the presence of the banyan tree or Kuber's mansion at the banks of Manasarovar referred to in the episodes, narratives, and tales contained in the ancient texts are products of an imaginative mind or something beyond ordinary imagination. Rather than undermining the importance of the spiritually-vibrant environment of Manasarovar and other holy lands, these texts through imaginative metaphorical expressions actually strengthen the experience-based ancient wisdom and enlightenment received by the sages and seers in these places.

In the literary traditions of Sanskrit, poetic expressions of the truth of the matter are taken to be figurative and are not to be evaluated in terms of factual depiction. Metaphorical and allegorical expressions most of the times are figurative and symbolic tools to convey the importance or attributes of the subject or object being described. They are also used to explain serious metaphysical issues many a time. In some old texts, Kashi is said to be a golden town sustaining on the trident of Lord Shiva. Lanka is said to be made of gold. What is sought to be conveyed by such expressions is the richness of these places in multiple ways. The presence of a pair of golden swans for instance in Manasarovar could allude to the beauty and sacredness of the place visited by a number of great souls and sages. Accomplished sages themselves are called great swans or *paramhansa* (परमहंस). It is said that in the unlimited world of creativity, a poet is the only creator. He creates what satisfies and pleases his imaginative mind. If the poet finds flavour in expressions of love, the whole world becomes romantic for him. But if he is detached, the passionate evocations of love convey little meaning for him:

अपारे काव्यसंसारे कविरेकः प्रजापतिः।
यथास्मै रोचते विश्वं तथेदं परिकल्प्यते।।

श्रृंगारी चेत्कविः काव्ये सर्वं रसमयं जगत्।
स एव वीतरागश्चेन्नीरसं सर्वं एव तत्।।

In Chapter 47 of *Vayu Purana* (वायु पुराण) and Chapter 121 of *Matsya Purana* (मत्स्य पुराण), geographical directions of Manasarovar have been given. Thus, this great holy lake is situated to the right of Mount Kailas and below Mount Vaidyuta:

कैलासदक्षिणे पार्श्वे क्रूरसत्त्वौषधं गिरिम्।
वृत्तकायात्किलोत्पन्नं मज्जनं त्रिककुट्प्रति।।

सर्वधातुमयस्तत्र सुमहान् वैद्युतो गिरिः।
तस्य पादे सरः पुण्यं मानसं सिद्धसेवितम्।।

Said to be enriched by a large variety of minerals, metals and natural medicines, Mount Vaidyuta seems to be the other name of Mandhata mountain ranges. The great Sanskrit poet Kalidas in his master-piece *Meghadutam* (मेघदूतम्) has made a clear mention about the location of Lake Manasarovar to the right of Mount Kailas before entering *Alaka Puri* (अलका पुरी). Through the main protagonist a *Yaksha,* a celestial attendant to Kuber who was the treasurer to the Gods, he tells the passing rain clouds whom he invites to be his messenger about the location of Lake Manasarovar. Though not directly relevant from a spiritual perspective, it would be of interest to explain the background of the storyline in brief:

The treasurer in the Kingdom of Indra in heaven, Kuber, lived in *Alaka Puri* situated to the north of Kailas. (Tibet, called as *Tribishtap,* is also known as heaven in some places of our mythological texts). Being a devotee of Lord Shiva, Kuber used to offer prayers to his beloved deity every morning with fresh lotus flowers, collected by a *Yaksha* (यक्ष), who served as his personal attendant, from a pond adjoining his house. One fine morning, a large black bee suddenly came out of a lotus flower when Kuber was offering these blooms in prayer and stung him on his hand. Disturbed and in pain from this unprecedented occurrence, Kuber investigated discretely into the matter. The Yaksha, though a loyal and careful help, was found to have changed his practice of plucking the lotus flowers from early in the morning to sunset during the previous evening. He would put them in water to maintain their freshness and prevent them from wilting. A large black bee that had gone to collect his feed (which is converted into honey later) had got trapped inside the lotus flower, which unfurls with sunrise enabling the bees to escape with their collection. The entrapped bee had thus stung Kuber in self-defence while escaping from captivity. Kuber also realized that the newly married Yaksha besotted in love and pre-occupied with his wife found it more expedient to delay his leaving home early every morning and switched to collecting the flowers the previous evening itself. Finding it an unacceptable negligence of duties, Kuber imposed an instant punishment of separation from his beloved wife for one year by banishing *Yaksha* to the distant earthly woods of Ram Giri Hills (Ramtek mountain in today's Maharashtra).

Yaksha in exile at Ramgiri hills spent the first eight months, in loneliness pining for his beloved wife, who too kept reminiscing about him day and night. With the onset of monsoons, he started wandering with the rain clouds finding the pain of separation and anxiety about the well-being of his wife unbearable. Without realizing their inanimate character, he begged the monsoon clouds to carry the message he yearns to relay in consolation to his beloved wife languishing far away in *Alaka Puri*. The Yaksha outlined the north-bound route to his destination in *Alaka Puri* in entrancing, pictorial, and bewitching detail to this lifeless messenger. He also warned him not to get trapped by the distractions and to quickly overcome all difficulties he was bound to face on the long journey. The imagery of Lake Manasarovar drawn by Kalidas in true poetic pencil through a lovelorn *Yaksha,* in the process of drawing up the detailed route with elaborations of the towns, sights, and splendours that would come his way, before reaching his home and the importance of his message to be conveyed to his beloved wife, underlines the exquisite beauty of this fresh water lake in the following words:

हेमाम्भोजप्रसवि सलिलं मानसस्याददानः
कुर्वन्कामं क्षणमुखपटप्रीतिमैरावतस्य।

धुन्वन्कल्पद्रुमकिसलयान्यंशुकानीव वातैः
नानाचेष्टैर्जलद ललितैर्निर्विशेस्तं नगेन्द्रम्।।

(O Cloud! after a taste of the dewy waters of Lake Manasarovar in which bloom the golden lotuses, spend a few moments there to get rid of your fatigue having travelled non-stop for so long. Cast your friendly veil on the elephant Airavata present there to bring smile to his face; and also shake the leafy clothes of the banyan tree standing nearby through your various posturing before reaching Mount Kailas.)

In the winter, the swans of Lake Manasarovar fly to other water bodies in distant locations with more hospitable conditions to avoid the cold climes of the Manas region. They undertake the journey back home to Manasarovar just before the onset of monsoon. Kalidas has, therefore, advised his inanimate messenger, lacking knowledge of his destination, to follow the swans returning to their natural habitat, namely, Manasarovar:

आकैलासाद् विसकिसलयच्छेदपाथेयवन्तः।
सम्पत्स्यन्ते नभसि भवतो राजहंसाः सहायाः।।

(On the way, flying with stalks of new shoots of lotus to satiate their hunger and eager to reach their natural habitat, namely, Manasarovar, royal swans in the sky will guide you to reach Mount Kailas.)

There are Gompas in the periphery of Manasarovar for Buddhist monks and preachers. These monasteries have been constructed by lamas or the Tibetan religious preachers from time to time. Since the forms and images of Manasarovar keep on changing from season to season, it is necessary to spend at least one whole set of seasons in one of these Gompas to internalize the changes in totality. This is quite difficult

Monasteries encircle Holy Manasarovar

Chiu/Jiu Gompa, perspectives and prospect

Thugolho (Qugu) Gompa, the chorten and the mani wall

Seralung Gompa, its Monastery

Gossul Gompa; Guru Rinpoche

Rakshastal, Ruins of its sole Tsepgye Monastery

Manas – hospitable to the solitary

Black-necked cranes, brown-headed gull, mud-plover, hoopoe, wheat-eater, pigeons, horned lark, red-billed crow

Royal swans of Manasarovar?

Rakshastal, beauty and power

Ellora Cave 29: 10-headed Ravan trying to lift Mount Kailas

Rakshas or Ravana Hrada *and the Divine, in one frame*

Two islands of Rakshastal; Source: www.mt-kailash.ru

for outsiders. Those who visit the Lake for a short time in a particular season can hardly see a fraction of what this great Lake represents, what to speak of comprehending the indescribable commanding beauty and grandeur along with the spirituality of this unique Lake.

The clear blue glacial waters of the Manasarovar, which incidentally remain frozen over for around eight months each year, are quite warming in body and spirit, not least because they are intrinsically knit with mythologies of different faiths and religions. Tibetans, who call it Mapam Tso, commemorate the lake to Milarepa's victory over a Bon shaman. The Buddhists believe that the Buddha's mother Maya bathed in this lake before conceiving him. Hindus believe that Manasarovar is the divine imaginative creation of Brahma, which is nothing more than a natural phenomenon for those who do not have the meditative insights and strength to grasp its spirituality. Linked to this is the ritualistic belief that those who bathe in the sacred waters of the lake, which is the abode of Lord Shiva, they will get cleansed of all sins from past and future lives.

No matter which way it is seen by the visitor, doubtless the 'Manasarovar is the ultimate natural sanctuary, blissful and quiet. It is here where the simplest of tasks generate so much inner balance, calm and happiness. The hours spent here ground and root you in a reality despite surreal narratives and takes from different faiths ringing in your ears. Frankly, the pilgrims spend a large part of their waking hours bathing in the lake, basking in the sun, watching the sun cast magical hues on the clouds dancing high in the sky, wondrously collecting shiny rounded pebbles with 'Om" engraved on them, taking longish walks along an unknown shore, seeking out the fauna and flora of the region, meditating, and other similar simple tasks. Night falls early. When the clouds disperse for unknown locales, visitors crane their neck thunderstruck by the most spectacular display of twinkling stars, playing out a harmony of music and lights one could never have imagined would sooth the senses at these high altitudes of solitude.

Many visitors step out between 3:00 a.m. and 5:00 a.m. to catch a glimpse of what they believe demi-Gods dancingly descending from heaven into the darkness of deep sacred waters of Manasarovar at *Brahma-muhurt* (ब्राह्म मुहूर्त). The snow-tops of the mountain ranges shimmer in the full-moon night at a distance carving out the boundaries of the amphitheatre of the Gods as they bathe, dance, play, and quite as suddenly go back to where they came from. The lights, twisting and turning, cavorting in abandon, are said to be deities, and it is not possible to shake the belief of the faithful with counters that these are perhaps a weather or scientific phenomenon. A very few do dare to recount that it is most likely luminous plasma which is created by a corona discharge from a sharp or pointed object in a strong electric field in the atmosphere around magnetic Mount Kailas, a weather phenomenon which in sea-farer's lore is called St. Elmo's fire.

Gompas around Manasarovar

There are eight Gompas built around Manasarovar, almost equidistant from each other, for Buddhist monks and preachers. Each is said to symbolise a spoke of the Buddhist Wheel of Life. Constructed mainly by lamas or Tibetan religious preachers from time to time, followers of the Buddha from the world over in search of enlightenment or salvation are found inhabiting these Gompas. All eight monasteries are stated to have been gutted during the Chinese Cultural Revolution. However, with the resumption of Indian pilgrimages and also other international tourism, five of these devastated Gompas and the monasteries have been partially restored starting from the early 1980s. It is also found that none of them attract the monks and preachers, pilgrims and visitors in quite the same numbers so far. The inhibiting presence of the Chinese military close to these cultural centres could be one important reason.

Thugolho/ Trugo (Qugu) Gompa, on the southern shores besides the serene Manasarovar, along with Chiu Gompa are perhaps the most active pilgrimage sites around Manasarovar where visitors stay for any period of time. It is about 7-hours walk away from Seralung Gompa, and has been a trading point for Tibetan nomads. The most revealing image of the holy Lake perhaps is the inscription on a stone in Qugu Gompa which conveys the following sense about the holy Lake Manasarovar:

> *"Lake Manasarovar (Mapam Yumtso) is the holiest of the holy places in the world. God himself sparkles in the centre of this lake in human form surrounded by one thousand lamas. All the lamas together in group sing prayers in his admiration explaining his divine attributes. This lake is the origin of four mighty rivers, namely, Karnali, Brahmaputra, Indus (Sindhu) and Sutlej in addition to four smaller rivers. Among the four mighty rivers, the first one contains hot water, second one cold, third one warm, and fourth one soft water. All the sins get washed away by taking repeated dips in this lake and forefathers also get liberated".*

Gossul Gompa perched high on steep cliffs, on the south-western shore of Manasarovar, is interestingly situated between the two lakes Manasarovar and Rakshastal at the narrowest part of the neck which is mainly solid rock. A bit south of the Gompa, driving up a ravine and some steep hills, the highest point on the neck between the two lakes is soon reached. From this vantage point, the view is indescribably picturesque and astonishes the mind to capture the vast and varied colour-scapes in the limited gross eye-frames.

Chiu/Jiu Gompa, sits on a steep red-coloured Sangtok Pelri Mountain. With the hot springs shooting out from the rocks below it which are thus full of vegetation of algae, the Gompa lies on the north-western shore of the magnificent Lake Manasarovar. The river or a natural canal Ganga Chhu flowing nearby connects Manasarovar with nearby Rakshastal. Chiu Gompa and Qugu Gompa can in fact be reached from each other through a continuous unbroken flat shoreline of the Lake. It is said that when Guru Rinpoche brought Buddhism to Tibet and left in 876 AD after having spent 54 years, he stopped at a cave to the west of Manasarovar and stayed there for a week. Chiu Monastery grew up around this cave, which also had a statue of Guru Rinpoche (Guru Nadrama). Jains and Bonpas equally revere this spot. The original monastery is said to be destroyed by the Chinese during their cultural revolution but a small monastery has been rebuilt which still houses its precious statues. The Mani Wall and the stones piled up were found to be engraved with words of law, calendar calculation, art theory, sutra texts and Buddha carvings.

Cherkip Gompa, the smallest of the eight, is in the north-west. It is said that the Buddha described a miraculous trip he took with 500 disciples north of Bodh Gaya to Cherkip. There, on a cliff overlooking Manasarovar, he found many caves in which he and his disciples undertook retreats. Later on, Cherkip and its caves became a retreat for Buddhists. Many of these caves have since submerged and in some hills near this monastery appear like disused south-facing meditation caves. The Gompa managed by the Drupka lineage of Bhutan was reportedly destroyed in the Cultural Revolution and has not been built since.

The original monastery of Langpona Gompa, to the north, was founded on a ridge shaped like an elephant's trunk, and was thus, called 'Elephant's Trunk'. It has been partially rebuilt in 1986.

Ponri or Bonri Gompa, on the north-eastern shore, was founded by Gugewa Khedrup Lozang Norbu who had studied at Sera Monastery, Lhasa. It belongs to the Gelug tradition, and its means "Bon Mountain" as it sits on a mountain which is holy to the Bon religion. Bonri Monastery has not been rebuilt.

Seralung Gompa, on the eastern shoreline, has a monastery called 'Pleasant Start' because of its beginnings as a resting place for Atisa. Atisa's most influential scholarly work, Bodhipathapradip, or Lamp for the Path to Enlightenment, lays down the Buddhist path in terms of the three vehicles-*Hīnayāna*, *Mahāyāna*, and *Vajrayana*. On the lake side by the monastery, one can find layers of sand in five colours – black, red, gold, green and silver.

Yerngo Gompa, on the south-eastern shore is now destroyed and in ruins. It was once consecrated to Guru Rinpoche. On top of a hill near the site is a chaktsal gang, which is a prostration site, and also a large mani wall.

The natural beauty of Manasarovar attracts the attention of saints, pilgrims, explorers, researchers, and inquisitive tourists spontaneously. Geographical and cultural identifications do not impede the visitors from internalizing the novelty of this mesmerising lake. This is the reason for all such visitors being uniformly impressed by its natural beauty. When the Swedish explorer Dr. Sven Hedin saw Manasarovar for the first time, he was wonderstruck by this unique creation of nature deep in the greater Himalayas to say, in his book '*Trans Himalayas*' published in the year 1909, that the lake's hyper-physical appearance generates ever-increasing curiosity and wonders which do not get satiated. He had no hesitation to say, "*I could live and die in this heavenly lake without ever growing weary of the wonderful spectacles always presenting fresh surprises*". In the year 1906, he spent over a month by the lakeside and pursued his research on the lake using a boat made of canvas to come to the conclusion that Brahmaputra, Indus and Sutlej rivers originated from Lake Manasarovar.

In a moving account on the landscape of Manasarovar, at page 151 of his book *ibid*, he writes,

> '*Wonderful, attractive, enchanting lake. Themes of stories, legends, play-ground of storms and changes of colours, apple of the eye of Gods and men, goal of weary yearning pilgrims, holiest of all lakes of the world, lakes of all lakes. Navel of old Asia where from four of the most famous rivers of the world, the Brahmaputra, the Indus, the Shatadru and Ganges rise of gigantic peaks surrounded by world of mountains, among which Kailas is the most famous of the world*'.

He also observed that while the outlines of Manasarovar and Rakshastal have been represented in very different ways in the course of time, Manasarovar has a very regular outline, almost round or a bit oblong, unlike Rakshastal which is irregular. His soundings also proved that Manasarovar is the deepest of all lakes in Tibet with two maxima at a depth of 65.0 metres in the eastern half and 81.8 metres in the deeper south-western half of the Lake.

Experiences and Experiments of Swami Pranavanand

Swami Pranavanand was one of most famous geographers of his time besides being a great saint. Born in 1896 in the East

Godavari district of Andhra Pradesh as Kanakdandi Venkat Somayajulu (his family-given name), he got his graduate degree from the DAV College Lahore in 1919. After working as an Accountant in the Railways for some time, he quit the job to join the freedom struggle and be a part of its non-cooperation movement. After functioning as an active member of the Indian National Congress for some years, he migrated to the path of spirituality acting upon his call of conscience and acute sense of detachment he developed towards the worldly life. He moved towards the Himalayas, the divine land of Gods and sages. He was initiated to renunciation by the great scientist saint Swami *Gyananandaji* (स्वामी ज्ञानानन्दजी) in the year 1926.

He wandered in the Himalayas for the next twenty-three years in search of the Truth. In addition to meditative practices, he pursued serious studies on other aspects of the Himalayas. The first visit he made to Kailas-Manasarovar was via Ladakh and Gartok in the year 1928. His second pilgrimage was in the year 1935 and this time he trekked through the access point in Gangotri-Nilang glacier. After the second pilgrimage, Swamiji continued his visits to Kailas-Manasarovar to pursue his *sadhana* and research work every year regularly. By the year 1948, he had performed 23 circumambulations of Kailas, 25 of Manasarovar and 01 of Rakshastal and 01 of Mandhata mountain range. He performed the circumambulations of lake Manasarovar 07 out of the 25 times in the winter with temperature falling to (-)25 degree Celsius with a layer of ice on the top of the lake 25 inches thick.

Swami Pranavanand, as stated in his book *Kailas-Manasarovar*, used to spend on an average two-to-six months every year after the year 1935 in Manasarovar region in connection with his research as well meditative practices. Through his scientific research, he demolished and modified some of the findings of Dr. Sven Hedin. His research involved available scientific tools, field verifications and study of relevant literature. His book is a unique piece of research work respected universally till date.

Using two boats, "*Janani*" and '*Janmabhoomi*", he studied various aspects of Manasarovar, Rakshastal and Gauri Kund, in different seasons, and also measured their respective depth and size. His findings are highly informative and of interest that make him one of the greatest contributors of knowledge on the geographical and cultural aspects of Tibet in general and Kailas-Manasarovar region in particular. His findings and important narratives have been borrowed in this book in many places with deep respect and gratitude. It would be of use to summarize his findings on Manasarovar for the benefit of readers who might not have been able to go through his book.

Manasarovar is a sweet water body with quality of water similar to those of rivers originating in the Himalayas. The great sage geographer Swami Pranavanand informs that situated at an altitude of 4,557 metres (14,950 ft.) from sea level, this lake appearing like a mini ocean with a circumference of 94.9 km (59 miles) and maximum depth of 91.44 metres (300 ft.). Its water is spread over 518 square km (200 square miles). The length of east, south, west and north coasts are about 25.75 km (16 miles), 16.09 km (10 miles), 20.92 km (13 miles), and 24.14 km (15 miles) respectively, and is about 24 km (14-15 miles) across.

Addressed as Tso-Mavang or Tso Mapham in Tibetan language, this attractive marvel of nature has been the centre of spirituality and cultural heritage of humanity belonging to multiple religious groups for centuries, besides being a unique geographic landmark. Sandwiched between two imposing mountains, Kailas on the north and Gurla-

Mandhata on the east, this natural creation appears tranquil even in turbulent weather. Another big lake, Rakshastal or *Ravan Hrada* or Langak-Tso in Tibetan language, is situated west of Manasarovar at a distance of about 6 miles. The spiritually-vibrant environment of Manasarovar offers peace and pleasure to the restless mind of even aimless wanderers. To those in pursuit of meditation, it provides the ambience for involution by focusing all energy and consciousness inwards in order to transcend to super-consciousness without distraction of meaningless, trivial, and worldly pursuits. In Jain religious texts, this lake is described as 'Lotus Heart' (पद्म हृदय) as if to justify its beauty to the core.

Kangari Karchhak, the Tibetan name of *Kailas Purana* (कैलास पुराण), contains an interesting episode, drawing from seven rows of trees around Manasarovar along with a number of mansions. The King of Serpents lives in the lake. The surface of this lake is in the shape of a curve. In the middle of the lake is a big tree enhancing its beauty. Fruits of this tree fall in the lake giving the sound of 'Jamb' which is why the surrounding land is called Jambuling. According to the Tibetan mythological tale, fruits falling from the tree in part are eaten by the King of Serpents residing in the lake. The unconsumed surplus ones reach the bottom, and get converted into gold.

In the Sabha Parva (सभा पर्व) of Mahabharata, Arjuna, the greatest warrior of his times, is stated to have visited Kailas-Manasarovar region in connection with his victory march or digvijaya (दिग्विजय) to assert the supremacy of the Pandava kingdom over other kingdoms. Yudhishthira, the eldest Pandava brother, desired to perform the Rajasuya Yajna (राजसूय यज्ञ), a prerequisite to assert control over other kings and sent his four brothers to the four directions. Arjuna, who went northwards got felicitated and was offered expensive gifts by local rulers, including supernatural beings, inhabiting this region. He is said have been overwhelmed to witness the grandeur of the inaccessible Meru mountain, with its golden and divine visage. To the right of the mountain, he finds a massive Jambu tree, evergreen with perennial flowers and fruits, which sustained sages and servitors through the ages. It was as though its branches were aspiring to reach the heaven.The narrative is clear that the whole surrounding area came to be known as Jambu-dwip (जम्बू-द्वीप) named after this famous evergreen tree:

मेरोस्तु दक्षिणे पार्श्वे जम्बूर्नाम वनस्पतिः।
नित्यपुष्पफलोपेतः सिद्धचारणसेवितः।

आस्वर्गमुच्छ्रिता राजन् तस्य शाखाः वनस्पतेः।
यस्य नाम्ना त्विदं द्वीपं जम्बूद्वीपमिति श्रुतम्।।

After taking a respectful circuitous walk around the Meru, Arjuna arrives at the banks of the Jambu river. He is entranced by the beauty of the river whose waters carried the taste of the fruits of the divine Jambu tree standing tall on its banks:

मेरुं प्रदक्षिणं कृत्वा पर्वतप्रवरं प्रभुः।
ययौ जम्बूनदीतीरे नदीं श्रेष्ठां विलोकयन्।।
स तां मनोरमां दिव्यां जम्बूस्वादुरसावहाम्।।

It is possible that being part of the larger region of what is described as Jambu-dwip (जम्बू-द्वीप) in ancient Indian texts and mythological literature, the area around Manasarovar is also thus called Jambuling. This could be another example of close cultural links between ancient India and Tibet. The shadow of Indian philosophical thoughts on the older Tibetan texts can be found in abundance. It is not for nothing that the supreme spiritual leader of Tibet, His Holiness the Dalai Lama calls India as Guru of Tibet.

In Indian literature, Manasarovar is described to be an integral part of the Himalayas like Mount Kailas. In the *Ramayana* of sage Valmiki, *Mahabharata* of sage Vyasa, various *Puranas*, and more so in *Manas Khand* of *Skanda Purana*, episodes related to Manasarovar are narrated in great detail. In Buddhist literature, Manasarovar is mentioned as '*Anotatta*' and '*Anavatapta*', which literally means that the water of this lake remains cold always. The importance of the tree in the middle of the lake is considered very special as its all-powerful fruits are said to cure all physical and mental ailments. Not only humans on earth, but Gods in heaven are also said to be interested to have a taste of these fruits.

Manasarovar, heaven on earth, more sacred to more people than any other, is mentioned also in the tales that large-sized lotus flowers bloom in the lake in the shape of Amitabh Buddha who represents unlimited powers. Lord Buddha and Bodhisattva used these flowers as their pedestal. Royal swans from the heaven come to Lake singing divine songs and skim and swim across its surface waters as though in complete enjoyment. In the hills around the lake, medicinal herbs are in thousands. Tibetan mythology eulogizes Lake Manasarovar variously and tales narrated above are indicative and illustrative.

Swami Pranavanand, on the basis of his empirical experience having lived in the Gompas and surveyed the lake round the year, wrote that the most thrilling view of Manasarovar could be witnessed only in the chilling winter. The whole lake is covered by a thick layer of ice during that period. With the arrival of the spring season, the frozen lake starts melting. The frozen ice cover melts with fierce scary shattering sounds and the molten melting lake suddenly appears in blue form with changing shades. This change in the lake presents an artistically adorable appearance, difficult to be described in words. Probably a great artist endowed with divine painting skill can only make attempts to draw it on a canvas, observes Swami Pranavanand.

In the distant past, apart from the Tibetan lamas, saints and pilgrims from India too had opportunities to stay in the Gompas around the lake to pursue meditative practices and during their pilgrimage to Kailas-Manasarovar. There are some permanent and semi permanent structures on the plains in front of the monasteries used for accommodation. While the atmosphere around Gossul Gompa appears a bit warmer, it is relatively colder around other Gompas. There are some smaller water bodies around Manasarovar. These include Yushup Tso in the south west, Tseti Tso in the west, and Kurkyal-Chhungo, Sham Tso and Ding Tso in the north and north east. According a Tibetan religious text, Lake Kurkyal Tso is the face or head of the divine Lake Manasarovar.

In the winter season in spite of appearing icy-beautiful, nature displays its most insensitive heart-breaking form with the death of thousands of fish in the lake and of hundreds of ducks, row upon row, on its banks. They just freeze to death. Similarly, the death of lambs born in the winter night in the vicinity shatter one's peace of mind with this callous cruelty.

With the arrival of spring season when the thick layers of snow start cracking, waves originating from the lake seem to convey that they could not remain suppressed for all the time. They rise to try to touch the sky and capture areas beyond the lake's territory in an abandoned expression of liberation from the bondage and cruelty of ice-chilled winter. The sounds of waves lapping gently in tune with the winds break the spooky lull of winter's retreat. The waves roar at times, when they relentlessly beat the shore-lands with oceanic might simply because the lands stood silently and watched the competitive game of nature played to the death. This is another play of the dancing nature.

In spite of the banks becoming sonorous due to waves, the deep middle of Manasarovar remains blissfully peaceful as if suggesting that Lord Shiva in the depths of his Samadhi there remains at peace and no amount of peripheral distractions can interrupt him. Its also as if Mount Kailas representing the Absolute Reality presents its shadow on Manasarovar from one side to make the lake bright and soulful. Mandhata hills from the other side add to its beauty by making it radiant like a crystal gem. Early in the morning during sunrise and in the evening at the time of sunset, Mount Kailas becomes golden. The Sun too in multiple shades of rich bronze seems to convey the message that greatness implies equanimity and steadfastness as the rise and fall do not change the true character and appearance of great souls:

उदेति सविता ताम्रस्ताम्रमेवास्तमेति च।
सम्पत्तौ च विपत्तौ च महतामेकरूपता।।

The visage of Manasarovar on a moonlit night is seen in an ecstatic reflection of the images of Kailas and Mandhata and their mountain ranges along with the moon itself in full bloom gracing the lake. Perhaps for a sincere seeker, no better environment for the realization of the Ultimate Reality can be found in this world. Naturally, this place was considered most conducive for meditative practices by sages and seers of all faiths, including followers of Jainism and Buddhism. Even an agnostic will find himself in a different world to experience the beauty of this incomparable lake presenting novelty, every now and then, unfailingly twenty-four hours a day.

It may however, not be appropriate to think that one could experience the beauty of this divine water body in totality immediately after stepping into Kailas-Manasarovar region. The lake seen in different moods from time to time under even a clear blue sky may belie the expectations of visitors due to an unpredictable weather in the region. Like the pilgrims, the clouds in the sky also appear to show their impatience to wrap themselves in embrace of the holy mountain of Kailas and to experience the bliss of a holy dip in Manasarovar. At times, it may not be possible to have a full view of Kailas and Manasarovar even after waiting for days altogether. The hypnotizing nature may sometimes indulge in the play of hide-and-seek with thick dense clouds engulfing up the mighty mountain and the fog challenging the pilgrims to catch a glimpse of the abode of Lord Shiva and his play ground including this holiest of the holy lakes. Nevertheless, sages, seekers, explorers, geographers, geologists, social scientists, philosophers, historians' artists, tourist etc. regardless of the degree of success in meeting their expectations have never lost interests in these two wonders of nature. This mesmeric heights of Kailas and unseen depths of Manasarovar have sustained for generations since the advent of time itself. Everyone gets overwhelmed and overawed after seeing them.

The pure and clean water of Manasarovar, like a shining blue sapphire, sometimes turquoise, aquamarine, azure blue, or even emerald green, on being touched energizes the enthusiastic pilgrims. They start enjoying its blissful magnetic effect instantly. Their hearts and minds get overwhelmed, as though wanting to surrender themselves wholeheartedly to the Ultimate Reality, while walking on its shores. Along with the dancing waves and waddling ducks in the shallow waters, pilgrims also find the shy woolly hare or mountain vole playing around the small shrubs and blowing whistles as if to break the soundless calm and peace of their surroundings. Sighting the rare swans and black-necked cranes, mud-plovers, snow-finches, along with the multitudes of brown-headed gulls and geese, besides many other fauna I could not recognize in and around the lake seems to suggest that like the seekers walking on the path of spirituality in the vibrant environment, the fauna too get enlivened by the vibrant and yet peaceful atmosphere of Manasarovar fearlessly ignoring the risks nor seeking the higher degrees of comfort elsewhere.

Overwhelmed by the wonders of Manasarovar, Dr. Sven Hedin had rightly observed more a century back:

> *"Manasarovar is the abode of sanctity and peace. No language on earth contains words foreseeable enough to describe the view from it over the lake. I enjoy the voyage to the full, for nothing I remember in my long wandering in Asia can compare with the overpowering beauty of this natural soil. Two flocks of gees are swimming on the water. All is so indescribably quiet, so ethical, transparent and transitory, so subtle and sensitive that I scarcely dare breathe. Wonderful, attractive, enchanting Lake Manasarovar is the pearl of all lakes of the world. To my dying day, I shall never forget it. I threw a farewell glance at the Manasarovar and experienced a feeling of bereavement at the thought that I must leave its shore".*

Indeed, it would not be a hyperbolic expression to say that filled with holy waters, this unique lake, venerated by the Gods themselves in *Ramayana*, *Mahabharata*, Puranas, across poetry and prose of various genres, reflecting surpassing beauty that is itself divine, emitting life-giving energy, and vigorous peace in the environment is the heart of nature in the purest form or a vibrant heaven on our earth. It is an oasis of infinite fullness and sublime purity, that is akin to the reflection of infinite consciousness in a pure mind. It resonates in body, mind, and soul as a seamless extension of the eternal flow of the ageless and timeless divinity. The architecture of nature was conceived here in the Kailas-Mansasarovar region on a bold and masterful plan. The unfolding beauty at every turn fascinates, entrances, bewitches, and fills the heart, mind and all the senses with a wonder at nature's crackling, silent magnificence.

Golden Lotus and Royal Swans

In the mythological texts and other forms of poetic expressions in ancient literature, in addition to age-old folklore of some religious groups, it is said that Manasarovar is adorned by golden lotuses besides the royal swans who can separate out water from milk. It is also said that the lake treasures pearls and all manner of precious gem stones. Verification of the ground reality by the gross eyes and other physical means seems not to support such descriptions, but wider reaching faith would have it otherwise.

It has earlier been explained that poetic truths and hyperbolic narratives in the mythological texts are means to attract attention of common man to the supernatural traits and serious metaphysical meanings. Expressions used to explain the context and underlying message have the potential to lead to incorrect conclusions if interpreted blindly, literally and independently. In given geographical and weather conditions, it is unthinkable to grow flowers in Kailas-Manasarovar without artificially creating conducive conditions. Words like 'lotus' and 'swan' are frequently used in spiritual contexts, and perhaps the great yogis could only explain what is sought to be exactly explained by the narratives suggesting presence of 'golden lotus' and 'royal swan' in Manasarovar. Sages who have liberated themselves from the cycle of birth and death are also described as swans in the spiritual texts. In the course of his stay to pursue research and meditative practices, Swami Pranavanand had tried to grow the lotus and many other flowering and non-flowering plants in the Manasarovar region but had not succeeded. He found remote, the possibility of the ancient sages living around Manasarovar.

Swamiji writes about the three varieties of aquatic birds in Manasarovar: The first variety is that of traditional swan called ngangba in Tibetan language. This class of birds with yellow bill, black knob at the tip and orange legs fly out of Manasarovar in October-November and visits places like Chilika, Malva, Surat and Mysore. They go back in March-April and breed in Tibet and Central Asia. The great Sanskrit poet Kalidas in his book Meghadutam seems to have referred to these swans as royal swans or Rajahansa (सम्पत्स्यन्ते नभसि भवतो राजहंसाः सहायाः). Elsewhere also it is stated that swans move back to Manasarovar when the clouds start roaming and roaring in the sky to indicate the onset of monsoon (जलधरसमये मानसं यान्ति हंसाः).

The second variety of birds are called ngaru serchung in the local language. Deep brown in complexion, this class of birds too comes to India but many of them stay back in Manasarovar even in winter.

The third variety is of gulls in deep grey colour, known as chakarma in the local language. Swamiji has explained main features of these birds in his book, which the more inquisitive readers may like to read.

In conclusion, there is no such bird called Royal Swan as understood by those believing in the literal meaning of mythological and poetic expressions. Such narratives are either products of imagination or convey meaning other than what is commonly understood by lay-persons and those believing in superstitions. It is also the case that the non-obvious is far more than what appears obvious.

Local people believe that swans are vegetarian. They subsist on eating the grass around Manasarovar. In spite of being non-vegetarian, Tibetans do not hunt or eat this bird as they consider her holy. However, they have no hesitation in collecting and consuming eggs of swans. Swans are seen roaming around in large number not only in Manasarovar but also in the neighbouring water body Rakshastal. The islands surrounded by the waters of Rakshastal are the reproduction centres as they are found conducive and safe for breeding by these birds. Therefore, swans are seen in larger number in vicinity of these islands. It becomes difficult for wolves to hunt these birds as the islands are inaccessible to them except when the lake waters freeze over. However, local people collect thousands of eggs from these islands to satiate their hunger.

The unending variety and beauty offered by Manasarovar has inspired and enriched the creativity of poets who associated divinity with everything related and relatable to this serene and magnificent lake. Gods and Goddesses of Indic religions are stated to be holding or sitting on lotus flowers produced in this lake. Manasarovar region being the play ground of Gods and Goddesses, it was natural to imagine existence of this flower in Lake Manasarovar to present its divine and distinctive attributes. Similarly, the continuously changing appearance of the lake overseen by snow-capped Kailas and Mandhata mountain ranges, rain-showering clouds gathering in different forms in the skies above the lake, reflections of rainbows, presence of a variety of birds including swans, etc presented the lake in such a beautiful and wonderous form that poets with imaginative minds found the supernatural in every natural phenomenon. The lake in their imagination became home of pearls and gem stones, and herbs found around were viewed as containing life-saving medicinal values. No scientific verification was required to do so in the poetic creation.

In conclusion, it is suggested that everyone visiting Kailas-Manasarovar should remain respectful towards this unique lake and do nothing to disturb its purity and peace. At times, it is seen that pilgrims in order to pay their respect for deities perform religious rituals on the shores of the lake as there are no structures called temples in Kailas and Manasarovar where such functions can be conducted. They leave plastic bags containing unused materials carried by them for rituals and wasted edible stuff behind, which contributes to the environmental pollution. Such actions even if they are unintentional and indeliberate on the part of pilgrims do not conform to their objectives of visiting the holy places. Pilgrims should, therefore, carefully conduct themselves and help in cleaning the place if earlier visitors are found to have left behind pollutants and other waste materials. Alternatively, a better option would be to avoid religious rituals and focus of meditative practices on the shores of the holy lake besides internalizing its uniqueness. Plastic bags or non-biodegradable packaging and other materials taken by the pilgrims should be consigned appropriately with the help of the local authorities or brought back for disposal rather than leaving behind.

Rakshatal frozen, and linked to Manas by Ganga Chhu

Winter freeze at Rakshastal, with an indulgent Mount Kailas

Artistic long fissures in the icy surface of Rakshastal

Ganga-Chhu, in various hues, bridging the two huge lakes

Four mighty rivers originate in Kailas-Manas environs

Sutlej (elephant-mouthed river Langchen Khambab), arising in Kanglung Kangari glaciers, weaves its way through 'Garuda Valley

Bokhar Chhu glacier, and many streams drain into the Indus, including the headstream Banggokong

Brahmaputra and Karnali

Awesome Brahmaputra, origin in glaciers; mysterious hidden falls; highest river in the world. Source: Shri Chandrashekaran

Origin of River Karnali

Shrub cinquefoil, mytnik, various-leaved snakehead, larkspur

Shy mountain voles, sharp-eyed lynx, heavy-haul yak, nimble mountain sheep, and wide canvas for wild donkeys: Wildlife in an inhospitable environment. Source: Some from the Web

8

Rakshastal or Ravan Hrada

From its western side, Manasarovar drains out its excess waters through *Ganga Chhu*, a channel which runs a distance of about about 6 miles, into another huge water body, variously named *Rakshastal* (राक्षसताल) or *Ravan Hrada* (रावणह्रद) or Langak-Tso in Tibetan language. Dr. Sven Hedin chronicles that Fakir Purana Poori of Banaras who had published his travelogue in 1792 AD, had called it "Lunkadh" or "Lunkadeh". In the map statedly drawn up by natives of the Manasarovar region for Emperor Akbar, which has been recorded around 1798 by the French Indologist, Abraham Hyacinthe Anquetil Du Perron, this Lake is referred to as "Lanka Dhe". William Moorcroft, the first Britisher known to have visited the region in 1812, called it Rawan Hrada. Interestingly, he recounts Sanskrit names of the principal streams that come from Kailas, which discharge themselves in Rawan Hrada, as *Shiva Ganga*, *Gauri Ganga*, *Darchen Gadrah*, and *Kaatyaayani*.

The total circumference of this deep blue lake has been estimated by Swami Pranavanand at about 199.4 square km (77 square miles) and its total water area is about 362.6 square km (140 square miles). The length of its east, south, west and north coasts is 46.6, 57, 73.8 and 22 km respectively. The maximum distance from north to south and east to west is 44 and 33.7 km respectively. The maximum depth of Rakshastal is estimated to be about half that of Manasarovar.

In *Manas Khand*, Rakshastal finds mention by the name of *Lanka Sar* (लंका सर). In Chapter 173, it is mentioned that river *Sharada* makes entry in this lake. River *Sharada* is reported to have appeared on the evocation of sage Pulastya, the grand-father of Ravan. According to this mythological narrative, *Sharada* originates from the beautiful valley just below Mount Kailas and its water makes Rakshastal replete and beautiful. It is stated that after the lake was filled up with the waters of *Sharada*, Ravan installed and consecrated a grand idol of Lord Shiva, whose great devotee he was, at the lake's centre and offered prayers to his grand father sage Pulastya and Lord Shiva. Vibhishan, the younger brother of Ravan, had secretly moved the river *Sharada* out of this lake with passage of time in order to purify the earth.

According to another legend, all Gods collectively had prohibited the demon king Ravan from taking a dip in Manasarovar. Therefore, he created another lake in his own name with the intention of garnering superpowers by pleasing his beloved deity Lord Shiva through acts of devotion, meditation and severe penance on its shores. It is held in Hindu mythology that upon the banks of one of the islands in this lake, he would make a daily offering with one of his ten heads as a sacrifice to Lord Shiva. Finally, on the tenth day, Lord Shiva was moved enough by his devotion to grant Ravan his wish to obtain superpowers.

In the sixteenth canto of *Uttar Khand* of Valmiki's *Ramayana*, there is an interesting tale in relation to Ravan's victory march. After defeating Kuber when Ravan was returning in his flying chariot, *Pushpak Viman* (पुष्पक विमान), which originally belonged to Kuber, suddenly the chariot came to a grinding halt near Mount Kailas. At this, Ravan's anger crossed its limit. In his angry tone, he sought an explanation from Nandishwar, a minion of Lord Shiva. On being told that Lord Shiva was engaged with his beloved Parvati at that point of time and did not like to be disturbed, Ravan's anger multiplied. He decided to unsettle the whole of Mount Kailas; the home of Lord Shiva. As soon as he tried to demonstrate his indomitable might and strength to uproot the mountain, all the living creatures there got frightened. Finding the mountain being shaken, Parvati held her lover and husband Lord Shiva by her hands tightly. To remove the source of Parvati's fright, Lord Shiva pressed the mountain with his toe. No sooner his toe touched the mountain, Ravan was crushed under the unbearable pressure, and cried out in pain:

पुष्करस्य गतिश्छिन्ना यत्कृते मम गच्छतः।
तमिमं शैलमुन्मूलं करोमि तव गोपते।।

एवमुक्त्वा ततो राम भुजान्निक्षिप्य पर्वते।
तोलयामास तं शीघ्रं स शैलं समकम्पत।।

ततो राम महादेव देवानां प्रवरो हरः।
पादांगुष्ठेन तं शैलं पीडयामास लीलया।
पीडितस्तु ततस्तस्य शैलस्तम्भोपमा भुजा।।

In his anger, Ravan had invested his entire energy to unsettle Mount Kailas. A stream of perspiration started flowing from his body the moment Lord Shiva's toe pressed the mountain. He remained in that position for one thousand years composing hymns in praise of Lord Shiva and continuously crying for relief:

संवत्सरसहस्रं तु रुदतो रक्षसो गतम्।

Finally, the magnanimous Lord of lords melted in mercy in the face of Ravan's pleas for relief. He liberated the king of demons who was one among his devotees and presented him a sword named 'Chandrahas' (चन्द्रहास) to bid him farewell.

It is because he cried (राव in Sanskrit means to cry) for 1,000 years, he was named 'Ravan' (रावण). After this incident Ravan led an austere life in deep meditation for a long time without leaving the place to please Lord Shiva.

Although this tale narrated in Valmiki's *Ramayana* does to make any mention of Ravan Hrada or Rakshastal, other legends associate the penance of Ravan to please Lord Shiva with the creation of this grand lake.

Rakshastal in the local language is known as Langak Tso, which means a water body in which there are five mountains. La means mountain, ngak means five and tso means lake. Lake Rakshastal, along with most of the lakes along the Tibetan plateau, is an endorheic lake, or sink lake, that normally retains water and allows no outflow to other external bodies of water, such as rivers or oceans, but equilibrate through evaporation. River Sutlej originates in the catchment areas to the west of Lake Rakshastal. As with any evaporative process, the minerals in the water stay behind and become more concentrated. Since Lake Manasarovar flows into Lake Rakshastal through Ganga Chhu, besides having four mighty rivers outflowing from it, the waters that leave take away the minerals it contains leading to a much lesser concentration left behind as new water flows in, and most importantly, out of that lake.

According to some Tibetan scriptures also, the surplus water of Manasarovar finds its outlet in Rakshastal. It is narrated that demons inhabited this lake, for which reason it was prohibited to others to drink its water. Once two golden fish living in Manasarovar quarrelled with each other, when the larger one drove the other out to Rakshastal in which process the Ganga Chhu, a canal of water, got created. In order to survive, she had to depend upon the natural canal,

Ganga Chhu to channelise the surplus waters of Manasarovar to Rakshastal. It is thus said that the waters of Rakshastal got purified and sanctified by the waters from Manasarovar and became a holy lake. After this development, people started drinking water from this lake.

Even so, some mysterious elements of the deep, darkness of Rakshastal linger. Many persons skirt this Lake, holding it in fear even to this day. Many pilgrims on my Yatra did not take a dip in its holy waters, preferring the freshness and good cheer of Manasarovar for their meditation and sojourns. However, many these days increasingly believe that it is as sacred as its sister-lake. As has been said by wise persons, even those powers which appear to be terrifying and destructive, or appear to have associations with the darker side of the central force, or even those like the Rakshastal are hidden in the darkness of its mysterious depths with linkages by popular lore to the *rakshsas* (राक्षस), are nevertheless as divine as those which we worship as embodiments of light, energy, goodness, and creativity.

After in-depth study of both the lakes Swami Pranavanand has observed that despite being smaller in size Rakshastal also is equally an ocean of beauty like Manasarovar. While the snow capped Gurla-Mandhata mountain ranges stand in the south and east of Manasarovar mainly sustaining the lake by feeding water, the eastern side of Rakshastal is a large high area of flat land (plateau). As there is no mountain to obstruct the winds blowing fast from the south, Rakshastal is far windier with a high chill factor in comparison to Manasarovar.

After observing both the lakes for a long time and undertaking his deep studies including research, Swami Pranavanand has underscored this fact that Rakshastal is shallower than Manasarovar. It gets frozen at least fifteen to twenty days before the latter in the winter season. The thick layer of ice in the lake also cracks two to four weeks before that of Manasarovar. The thickness of ice layer in the winter on this lake is two to four feet. This feature of Rakshastal is attributable to the fact that unlike Manasarovar which faces Gurla-Mandhata mountain range in the east, there is no such mountain to its east which could serve to obstruct the biting winds blowing from its south.

There are seasonal changes in the appearance of Rakshastal too as in Manasarovar which makes it a thrilling experience to see it at different points of time throughout the year. After the ice cover melts, speedily blowing early morning winds make the sonant shores of Rakshastal with its forceful waves spreading foam on the shoreline extremely attractive and scary in its sheer ferocity. The lake appearing disturbed becomes calm after some time. It's appearance changes to a shining green emerald and its peaceful and serious ambiance no more terrifies. The small pebble stones and fish swimming just below its surface become clearly visible. Ducks on the shores and friskiness of mountain voles blowing whistles while hiding in the shrubs present a very pleasant and innocent eco-system in and around this lake. It becomes a life-time experience of a different world for pilgrims altogether. Lachato, an island in Rakshastal is a nesting ground for wild geese. The birds' nest and lay eggs in thousands knowing well that the summer waters will protect them from becoming prey to man or beast. But with the advent of winter freeze, egg gatherers cross over the frozen lake to harvest all the eggs.

Even though no natural shield of mountains is available to Rakshastal from its southern and eastern sides as we find in Manasarovar, one could still see a magnificent distant view of the snow peaks of the Gurla-Mandhata mountain ranges from table-lands along its shores.

Mount Kailas with sublime majesty and serenity in the north of Rakshastal contributes to its grandeur immensely making it simply indescribable. All the streams originating from southern Kailas find their destiny in this lake, making it a massive perennial water body and distinctly different from the neighbouring Manasarovar. The total area of this lake becomes extremely difficult to measure considering that there are two sizeable islands inside with their rough and bumpy landscape. It is for this reason Dr. Sven Hedin even after spending more than one month in this area got confused and ended up wrongly concluding that there were three islands inside Rakshastal, writes Swami Pranavanand. His findings were demolished, and corrected subsequently to two islands in Rakshastal by the sage geographer Swamiji after years of sustained research.

River Shatadru or Sutlej originates from north-west Rakshastal although no physically-verifiable outlet to show the release of water is found. As has been noted by Swami Pranavanand in his book, a few streams on the left side of the origin of this river make their entry in this river. This has created confusion in the minds of many researchers leading them to believe that Rakshastal can not be source of river Sutlej in the absence of any outlet to form the river.

Two Islands of Rakshastal

Dr, Sven Hedin had written about the existence of three Islands inside the Rakshastal. This was discounted by Swami Pranavanand after he physically verified entire lake from all sides, besides touring the two Islands, before writing about them. Called Lachato and Top-Serma, Swamiji had inspected both in winter after the surface of the lake had frozen with a thick layer of ice, travelling to them on a yak.

According to his description, Lachato is in the shape of a tortoise. Its neck surrounded by water from three sides stretching towards a peninsula on the southern shore of Rakshastal. The distance between the neck and the spike land facing it is about 0.8 km. The circumference of Lachato is about 1.6 km. This rocky Island has a heap of white stones on its top. There are enclosures made of stones in the eastern and western part of the Island for egg gatherers.

Swamiji mentions about a group of swans noticed by him on north-eastern side of this Island during his visit. The egg-gatherers of Kardung village which is situated near Rakshastal come to this Island riding on their yaks in the last week of April for their harvesting of eggs, when the Tal is capped by a thick layer of ice. With the approaching spring season such forays over ice can be treacherous, and the ice has been known to crack-up suddenly taking the egg-gatherer, the eggs and the yak into the icy depths of the Rakshastal. Obviously, in case the ice melts after they reach the Island, they get held hostage on it somehow surviving on the flesh and eggs of birds, and perforce have to wait out for the next winter and the ice to form before returning home.

Top-Serma is also full of rocks like Lachato. Much bigger in size, its southern end is known as Tonak. About a mile long from east to west, the width between its north and south ends is 1.2 km. Swamiji has mentioned about a broken structure or house on the eastern side. According to the locals, a Buddhist preacher is reported to have lived there some time back, travelling to the mainland only to procure food and other provisions during winters, while performing meditation in utter solitude during the remaining part of the year. A clay image of Chenresig (Avalokiteshvara) had been collected by Swamiji from the ruins of this house as a memento of his visit to this Island.

Ganga Chhu

It is clearly seen that Manasarovar and Rakshastal are two separate water bodies. While most of the streams leading to Manasarovar have their source in the Gurla-Mandhata mountain ranges in the south east, the Rakshastal is formed from the streams originating in the slopes of Mount Kailas in the north. After circumambulating Manasarovar 25 times, Swami Pranavanand supports this assumption that Manasarovar and Rakshastal formed a single unified lake in the distant past. The single huge lake would have divided into two due to geographical changes in the course of time. Swamiji came to this conclusion after finding the surplus water of Manasarovar flowing into Rakshastal through Ganga Chhu, which looks more like a naturally formed canal. The water filtering and flowing from the north-west side of Rakshastal forms river Sutlej. Like-wise the excess water of Manasarovar drains into Rakshastal through a natural canal. There is no other way for movement of the surplus water of Manasarovar.

Ganga Chhu is about 6-mile long, 40 to 100 feet wide and 2 to 4 feet deep. The sage geographer has mentioned that he had crossed this natural canal forty-four times during his long stay in the Manasarovar region.

Through his profound piece of research, Swamiji also refuted the popular belief that Manasarovar was the origin of Indus and Brahmaputra rivers. Swamiji concluded that it was ignorance that resulted in the assumption that river Indus originated from the northern or southern sides of Mount Kailas and that the original source of the river Sutlej was Gauri Kund situated on its south-west slopes.

Contrasting Rakshastal and Manasarovar

Both lakes are unique manifestations of nature and have caught human attention world-wide. There are many legends associated with them, even as ancient texts of Tibet as well as of India give various descriptions. Swamiji has highlighted the contrasts between them in his book as summarised briefly below.

Although it starts snowing from the month of September onwards, Manasarovar starts freezing and gets covered by the thick layer of ice after mid December, turning fully white and appearing like curd towards the end of the month. None attempts to walk over its frozen surface, neither on foot nor by yak. The layer of ice with thickness of about two feet remains its outer cover till April. It melts towards the end of April or in the first fortnight of May. In contrast. Rakshastal freezes over two to three weeks before Manasarovar. Ice layer of this lake, which is two to four feet in thickness starts melting two-three weeks after Manasarovar. Some winter activity is seen by the local people on its icy surface, unlike complete stillness at Manasarovar. Fierce sounds are heard emanating from the lake when the frozen ice covering Manasarovar starts cracking up in spring. However, similar terrifying and ferocious sounds from the Rakshas are rare.

The shoreline of Manasarovar is replete with eight Gompas. Only one, Tsepgye Gompa, is seen to exist about 2.5 km from the shoreline of Rakshastal towards its north-westerly direction. Swamiji recounts that in 1941 when the monastery's inmates fought off an attack by a band of Kazakh warrior nomads, who were on a spree with a few hundred others to sack and loot e monasteries and habitats in Western Tibet. The fight put up by the inmates at Tsepgye diverted the attention of marauders and prevented further decimation of Purang valley. They reached up to Ladakh, gathering a massive amount of loot from there. However, it is chronicled that here they were apparently given an honourable entry into India by the British authorities, and settled somewhere in north west frontier. However, the monastery appears to have been further destroyed during the Cultural Revolution, Only the ruins remain.

While the total area of Manasarovar is 518 square km, the waters of Rakshastal extend for 388 square km. The depth of Manasarovar is twice that of its once twin lake. One is rounded, an oblong, in shape, the other wickedly irregular. In terms of natural beauty both the lakes are comparable, but in terms of spiritual and religious importance, Manasarovar is incomparable. Gurla-Mandhata mountains shield Manasarovar from the strong winds blowing from the south, enabling it to remain calm and in control of its waves. Rakshastal presents the opposite. Strong winds blowing from the south are experienced, disturbing its tranquillity through noisy waves. Perhaps, this is also the reason for the shores of this lake appearing colder. Early freeze and late melt are also attributable to the same factor.

Swami Pranavanand found his experience of watching Manasarovar and Rakshastal at the time of melting snows far more wonderful and thrilling than his experience of watching them at the time of freezing. Both the lakes seem to remain eager to touch the feet of the holy deity Mount Kailas and the sparkling Gurla-Mandhata through rising waves as if to convey gratitude to them for their existence. In the night with clear sky, Manasarovar in the greenish blue colour with reflections of the bright moon and Kailas and Gurla-Mandhata mountains on the north and south presents its ecstatic form to give a flavour of divinity. Its vibrant and spiritually charged environment overwhelms the hearts of seekers and ordinary visitors without discrimination. The thrill and the bliss experienced are simply stupendous, quite extraordinary.

9

Four Mighty Rivers from Kailas-Manas Region

Like many rivers passing through the length and width of various regions in India from their respective source to their final destination, such as Ganga, Yamuna, Sarayu, Narmada, Krishna, Godavari, and Cauvery, the four great rivers, namely, Indus, Brahmaputra, Sutlej and Karnali originating from Kailas-Manasarovar region are equally associated with sacredness. There are many legends and narratives about the original sources of these rivers in the ancient Indian and Tibetan literature and lore which speak volumes about their sanctification and veneration.

Some holy texts in India and Tibet describe Kailas and Manasarovar as the main source of these rivers. Swami Pranavanand studied the religious texts and physically and scientifically verified their veracity. Without hurting religious sentiments of any group, he thus successfully removed the confusion about the river-origin. Before demystifying the narratives, he describes an interesting tale from the Tibetan Kailas Purana, using names largely identical with Puranic ones of four waters that flowed from Mount Meru, as follows:

"*The Tibetan Kailas Purana says that the Ganga had at first descended from Kailas to the spring Chhumik Thungtol; that four rivers emerged out of this spring in copper pipes through the lake Manasa; that*

> *(1) Ganga came out of the elephant-mouth (Langchen Khambab, Elephant-mouthed river, or Sutlej) near Dulchu Gompa on the west and went to Chhemo Ganga in Gyagar (India);*
>
> *(2) Sindu went northwards in the beginning and came out of the peacock-mouth (Mapcha Khambab, Peacock-mouthed river or Karnali) at Mapcha Chungo to the south in Lankapuri and proceeded westwards to Sindu-yul;*
>
> *(3) Pakshu or Vakshu went westwards in the beginning and thence came out of the horse-mouth (Tamchok Khambab, Horse-mouthed river, or Brahmaputra) from a mountain in Chem-yungdung to the east, went to Chang (Tashi-Lhunpo) and thence to Kamarupa in India, where it is called Lohita; and*
>
> *(4) Sita went southwards in the beginning and thence came out of the lion-mouth (Senge Khambab, Lion-mouthed river or Indus) from a mountain called Senge, situated to the north of Kailas and went to Baltichen and Changhor".*

It is narrated that the water of river Sutlej is cool, drinking which gives the strength of an elephant, and its sands contain gold. The water of Karnali is warm, drinking which brings out peacock-like beauty, and its sands contain silver. The water of Brahmaputra is cold, drinking which brings the sturdiness of a horse, and its sands contain cat's eye. The water of Indus is hot, drinking which brings out the heroic spirit of a lion, and its sands contain diamonds. It is said that all four rivers after circling Kailas and Manasarovar seven times, proceed in westerly, southerly, easterly and northernly directions respectively. In reality, all four rivers are within a distance of 45 km from Manasarovar's shores.

Sutlej - Elephant-mouthed Langchen Khambab

Tibetan religious texts and traditions say that river Sutlej originated from Dulchu monastery near Rakshastal which is situated at a distance of 63 km (39 miles) from the western end of Manasarovar or Rakshastal. *Kangari Karchok*, the Kailas Purana of Tibetans, describes the sacred elephant-mouthed river or Langchen Khambab as a long and extensive river that rises from the 'lake unconquerable', the Tso Maphan or Manasarovar.

The source of Sutlej traced by Swami Pranavanand lies in the red coloured mountains of the Kanglung Kangri glaciers located about 48 km (30 miles) easts of Manasarovar. Langchen Khambab finally reaches Rakshastal giving birth to river Sutlej. The landscape has been eroded into fantastic shapes by wind, rain and winter torrents. The earth forests of Tholing and Tsparang of the Gugi Kingdom through which it channels its way are full of huge columns, pillars and buttresses formed by rocks that collectively appear like a forest from afar, an out-of-this-world landscape formed by geological movements many millennia since. The Kanglung ruins stand revealed on the northern bank of Sutlej, in what was once called 'Garuda Valley' by ancient Zhangzhung civilisation of western Tibet.

The mighty Sutlej enters Himachal Pradesh through Shipki La gorge at 12,894 ft. cutting across the formidable Zanskar, Greater Himalayas, and Dhauladhar ranges. After a journey of 1,445 km traversing also through Punjab, it drains into the river Indus in Pakistan. The Sutlej basin is home to two National Parks and 32 wildlife sanctuaries, including India's largest one (Harike Bird Sanctuary) located at its confluence with the river Beas.

Indus - Lion-mouthed Senge Khambab

The original source of river Indus, known locally as Senge Khambab, is Bokhar Chhu glacier to the north-east of Mount Kailas at a distance of about 100 km (62 miles) from Manasarovar. This region drains the largest number of glaciers and mountain slopes of Karakorum, Zanskar, Ladakh, and Himalayan ranges. A large number of streams originating from the glaciers of Mount Kailas feed into Senge Khambab or the Lion's mouth. The perennial headstream, Banggokong, is about 30 km away from the place that Dr. Sven Hedin believed was the source of the Indus.

The Indus flows in a constricted valley north-westward through Tibet, entering Ladakh where it follows a long nearly straight course between the Ladakh range and the Zanskar range. The confluence with the mighty Zanskar river which has more water than the Indus at this point is just below Leh. Suruand Dras are the other left bank tributaries which join the Indus near Kargil. Moving north-westward, the Indus is joined by Shyok-Nubra tributaries, which arise from the Siachen Glacier in Karakoram Range. River Shigar and Gilgit, another important tributary, join it from the west. Downward the Indus crosses the central Himalayan range through a huge synclinal gorge, passing by Nanga-Parvat. It turns south-west to enter Pakistan and then cruises south-ward into the Arabian Sea having travelled for 2,885 km.

Brahmaputra, Horse-mouthed Tamchok Khambab

The geographical source of Brahmaputra river, known in Tibet as Yarlung Tsangpo, as noted by Swamiji is in Chema Yung-dung glaciers and frozen lakes situated about 63 km from Manasarovar on its south-east in the vicinity of the revered 'Kailas' spur. Various streams originating from these glaciers put together form this largest river in the Indian subcontinent.

A part of stunning natural features in Tibet, this 4,696 km long river runs through the mysterious Yarlung Tsangpo Grand Canyon (the world's deepest, longest, and highest river canyon), before entering Arunachal Pradesh. When the river flows eastwards on the Tibetan plateau, its average gradient is a mere 15 feet per mile. But it suddenly makes a full left turn and starts flowing northwards towards the eastern edge of the Great Himalayan range.

Interestingly, here the river confronts two Himalayan peaks 'Namcha Barwa' and 'Gyala Peri'. The canyon here, only about 13 miles wide, is said to have a maximum depth of 5,300 metres and is thus fondly called the 'Mount Everest of Gorges'. The waters terrifyingly crash down in this gorge. After this great fall, also called the 'Hidden Fall', the river now makes a full about-turn to the south and rushes towards Arunachal Pradesh, in the 'Great Bend' of almost 270 degrees. The Hidden Falls, described by Guru Padmasambhava 1,200 years back and which have eluded almost everyone else, are anyway impossible to approach because of the steep shear edges along the gorge. Tibetans consider this Great Bend region as a most-revered heavenly abode of Gods. Ancient Tibetan texts (Neyigs or guides to sacred places) describe a paradise or Beyul behind the great fall, which one can approach through a secret door.

In another marvel of nature, the river falls down, in a series of trickly falls, at an unbelievable slope of 50 to 200 feet per mile creating a tremendous force. The steep banks are covered with dense forests which are practically impregnable. China opened up access to this region for explorers only in 1990, and now only the last 5-mile patch still remains to be fully explored.

Karnali - Peacock-mouthed Mapcha Khambab

Karnali river's original source has been traced by Swami Pranavanandji in the Lampiya pass. The river takes its shape from the main spring that originates from Mapcha Chungo situated at a distance of 30 km south-east of Manasarovar. It cuts through the Himalayas in Nepal and joins river Sharda at Brahmaghat in India. Together they form river Ghaghara, the largest tributary of the Ganga by volume and the second longest by length after Yamuna. The total length of Karnali up to its confluence with the Ganga in Bihar is 1,080 km (670 miles). Lower Ghaghara is also known as river Sarayu which is mentioned in *Ramayana*. Ayodhya is situated on its right bank.

Mythology deepens the Mystery

Tibetan mythological descriptions about the origin of these rivers in a larger sense, and those in ancient Indian texts tracing them to Kailas-Manasarovar region is not very far from the reality if the tales woven around them are not taken in a literal sense. The rivers' origins in reality are within an aerial distance of about 45 km from Manasarovar.

There is an interesting description in Valmiki's *Ramayana*. In the twenty-fourth canto of Balakanda (बालकाण्ड), it is said that when Vishvamitra along with Rama and Laxman reached the banks of river Ganga, the seekers of spirituality and their masters gave an advice to them for their safe travel. They arranged a sturdy and beautiful boat for their onward journey. After boarding the boat and reaching in the middle of the stream, Rama suddenly heard loud pounding. He became curious to know the cause and wanted to be enlightened by his teacher. Sage Vishvamitra explained about the creation of divine lake Manasarovar which was the source of the Sarayu flowing by the side near Ayodhya and that the pounding sound was generated when this river with its force was hitting the river Ganga at their confluence:

तस्मात्सुस्राव सरसः सायोध्यामुपगूहते।
सरः प्रवृत्ता सरयूः पुण्या ब्रह्मसरश्च्युता।।

Needless to say, that river Karnali with its original source around Manasarovar is known as Ghagara when it enters India through the Bahraich district of Uttar Pradesh. Subsequently this river meets Sharada and both these rivers in combination assume another name- Sarayu when it passes through places by the side of Ayodhya - remains so till its assimilation in the Ganga in Bihar's Chhapara district. All her previous names are left behind and the river becomes part of the Ganga.

In conclusion, it is apparent that the original sources of these rivers are not very far from the Manasarovar region. Probably, all the rivers originating from this region are stated to be originating from Kailas or Manasarovar in the ancient mythological texts of Tibet and India. Tibet had very close trading and cultural ties with India since time immemorial. The ancient Tibetan literature in style and content has been deeply influenced by the scriptures composed in India. That is why the similarity in many mythological narratives. It would be desirable not to interpret the mythological and legendary narratives regarding the original sources of these rivers in literal sense and grasp them in real sense which seem to be in conformity with the ground reality.

It may also be relevant that river Kali with its original source in Lipulekh retains its name after getting united with several of its tributaries. It meets river Sarayu originating from Nandakot in a place called Pancheshwar on the Indo-Nepal border. The combined river becomes Sharada near Tanakpur. It becomes Sarayu again after getting united with

Karnali which becomes Ghaghra when the river enters India in Bahraich district in Uttar Pradesh. Therefore, there should no discrepancy to trace the origin of Sarayu in Manas region as stated by sage poet Valmiki in his *Ramayana*. Coherent interpretation of mythological narratives is in conformity with the literary and Pauranic traditions.

Flora, Fauna and Natural Resources

It can be said to be ironical that despite being home of four mighty rivers and two massive lakes, in addition to several streams, vegetation is sparce and fauna are scarce in Kailas-Manasarovar region. Sitting by Manasarovar, throughout the day flocks of geese, grebes, and gulls were plentiful to have the company of, and even the rare crane and red-billed crow were sighted. Some other waders bobbed along on its turquoise blue waters, and one did not have to strain to see a rich harvest of fish, carp, and scale-less loaches swimming in the waters.

Plant species, associated with the flora of the deserts of neighbouring Central Asia and species of mesophytic habitats of East Asia, are seen to appear generally after the glaciers have retreated in the western and north-western parts that we travelled through. Due to the topography and arid climate, trees and larger plant forms were absent, but some grasses and in scattered areas some salt-tolerant shrubs and wormwood were found growing. On the slopes of Kailas various varieties of creeping plants were seen, while in the valleys of Gurla-Mandhata, a species of red-horned tree growing up to 4-5 ft was seen.

Tibetan garlic (gokpa), batuwa (livu) and nettle (*bichhu-ka-buti)* were found grow everywhere. Some varieties of mushrooms, both edible and inedible, grow in the vicinity of Manasarovar. Also, in the area of this lake and near the river Gurla and in some other places, a medicinal plant called *lal-buti* (red grass) whose leaves turn red in October is seen growing up to a height of no more than 60-80 cm. against typhoid and fever. A wonderful medicinal plant called tuma (suma) grows on Manasarovar's shores.

Notwithstanding the vibrant life forms in and around Manasarovar, besides the burly yak, horses, and donkeys, a few wild blue mountain sheep, voles and hares were also sighted. In the absence of green cover on the Tibetan plateau, herbivorous wild animals in particular are seen to be smaller in size and as if suffering from deprivation. Ancient scriptures speak of the lotus, kalpavriksha, golden swan, peacocks, airavat-haathi, nandi, and otherwise also plentiful flora, fauna, fishes, birds, insects, and other life forms at Kailas-Manasarovar, including Himalayan cedars under which the deities sat.

It could be argued that climatic and topographic conditions were less harsh in their pre-glacial distant past. How are we to interpret this unkind face of nature on what appears an excellent, pleasant and blissful experience in and around the two lakes Rakshastal and Manasarovar? In 2004, the lakes together were designated as a singular Ramsar wetland complex—a globally recognized designation accorded to wetlands of global importance. At the time of Kailas parikrama, wild animals seen occasionally can hardly be said to be healthy although that is the best period of the year for them in terms of amiability of weather.

Apart from its spiritual significance, the region has also been famous for its yield of gold and turquoise, though most of the mines in surrounding hills stand abandoned. The region brought many curious western explorers, including game lovers William Moorcroft, Hyder Hearsey, explorers Sven Hedin and the pundit surveyors. Its most famous pilgrim Swami Pranavanand visited more than ten times, carried out scientific surveys, collected data and penned multiple guidebooks. I salute them for enriching generations to come with the fruits of their explorations and studies.

10

Kailas

Mount Kailas, the holiest of holies, stairway to heaven revealed from its distinctive conical appearance, remote and mostly inaccessible to the bulk of mankind, is located in Western Tibet (elevation, 6,638 metres; 21,771 ft). Its peak majestically rises and dominates over the rest of the range. Interestingly, Lake Manasarovar, equally sublime and containing mysterious depths and hues, appears as if its inseparable half. Together, they conjure the image of a temple with its presiding adored deity, and the lake full of molten shimmering mirror-like waters, the focus of deep reflection. Pali literature speaks of *Kelasa* situated around Lake Anotatta in *Himava* (Himavan) as the highest peak of silver colour bent inwards "like a crow's beak".

The sacred mountain has the shape of a tetrahedral pyramid, whose lateral sides are turned towards four cardinal points. It consists of thirteen horizontally spaced stepped layers, topped with a cap of eternal ice. Its south side-wall is cut from top to bottom by an impossibly straight cleft that runs exactly in its middle. Layered terraces appear as though a huge stone staircase is leading from the base of the mountain to its very top. Sunrise, and rays of a setting sun, give this natural design a similarity with a left-sided swastika. Satellite or high-resolution imagery show that it resembles eight petal flowers on the map. Mount Kailas, or Kang Rinpoche, is thus considered one of the world's most sacred mountains. Four major rivers of Asia – Indus, Sutlej, Brahmaputra, and Karnali – originate in the four cardinal directions in its environs. It is a sacred destination for pilgrimage and parikrama for Hindus, Jains, Buddhists and Bonpos. For Hindus, it is the abode of Lord Shiva. For Jains, it is the place where the first Tirthankara Bhagwan Rishabhadeva attained enlightenment. Tibetan Buddhists believe it is a dwelling place of the Demchok (*Chakrasamvara*) and for Bonpos, it is a nine-storeyed left-opening swastika mountain, a seat of spiritual power.

These associations have served to uphold Kailas' mythological, cosmological and astrological identity, also depicted as Mount Meru, the Centre of the Universe and "Navel of the Earth" or axis mundi. At its core is the Ultimate Reality or Lord Shiva – without beginning or an end. Hardly surprising that what is commonly understood as the Hindu view of life echoes similar existential thoughts. The universe, cyclical in its manifestations, comes into being and passes away according to a regular pattern, not unlike inhalation and exhalation, again without an end.

Die-hard believers from amongst these faiths have also imagined the affinity or association of hundreds of temples and mountains with Kailas including across large parts of Asia. In fact, it has been a common denominator embodying and symbolizing the Hindu world-view at its deepest level of sub-consciousness.

Hindu Religious Geography and Kailas

Mount Kailas has inspired the greatest architectural and artistic achievements in Hindu Asia. Among the most iconic ancient temples associated with it are the Kailasa Temple at

Sacred Kailas – Far reach; Associated holy mountains

Sacred temples: Kanchi Kailasanathar; Kailasa, Ellora Caves; Prambanan, Java, Indonesia; and Baphuon, Angkor, Cambodia.

Solitude, Austerity of Cave-Dwelling around Kailas-Manasarovar

Darchen: Panoramic view of Gurla-Mandhata and Barkha Plains

Parikrama of a life-time: Magnificient Kailas

The Divine Kailas from Barkha Plains;
Kailas' Faces up close - North, East, South, and West

Ashtapad where Bhagwạn Rishabhadev attained salvation

Outer Parikrama, Gompas, Symbolism, Sublime Nature

Four beautiful Monasteries around Kailas – Chuku and its Conch Shell; Diraphuk; Zutrul-phuk; distinctive architecture of Gyangdrak – and Saptrishi Caves; Source: Unknown from the Internet-Web

Kangnyi Chorten; Tarboche; Yam Dvar: Gateway for Salvation

Glimpses from the kora of Lha Chhu Valley after Yam Dvar to Drira-phuk with an array of Chortens lining the way

Ellora Caves and Kanchi Kailasanathar Temple both in India, Prambanan or Rara Jonggrang in Indonesia and Baphuon in Cambodia.

In the Gita, Lord Krishna identifies himself with the Himalayas (स्थावराणां हिमालयः) and Mount Kailas (मेरुः शिखरिणामहम्). In Manas Khand, Kailas is where Lord Shiva and Goddess Parvati live together. In Brahmanda Purana, Vayu Purana, Matsya Purana, Shiva Purana, Bhagavata Purana, Vishnu Purana, etc, detailed descriptions are found of Kailas, and its location and attributes. Other Puranas and a large body of literature are replete with references of Kailas in different names and specialties. There is complete unanimity in all texts that Lord Shiva is the presiding deity of Kailas which also houses Kuber, treasurer of Lord Indra in Heaven. It may be of interest to cite a few references from some mythological texts in relation to Mount Kailas here.

Indicating the geographical location of Mount Kailas, *Brahmanda Purana* says that behind the Himalayas in the centre is the mountain called Kailas. Kuber lives there with his servitors, the *Yakshas* (a class of supernatural beings). The river of Gods in heaven established herself with a sense of belongingness in the long coiled hair on the head of Shiva who was in a trance on Mount Kailas, on her landfall before moving earthwards.

मध्ये हिमवतः पृष्ठे कैलासो नाम पर्वतः।
तस्मिन्निवसति श्रीमान्कुबेरः सह गुह्यकैः।।1/2/1।।

मदीया इति निश्चित्य समाहितमनाः शिवे।
तत्र त्रिपथगा देवी प्रथमं तु प्रतिष्ठिता।।1/2/27।।

Similar descriptions are seen in the Adi Parva (आदि पर्व) of *Mahabharata* while describing the hermitage of sage Vashishtha (वशिष्ठ) by Mount Kailas and in *Matsya Purana.*

The latter states that on the north of his *Ashram* is Mount Kailas greatly enjoyed by Lord Shiva, the killer of demon *Tripura*. This mountain is adorned by crests having a variety of divine trees. There is a lake in this mountain, which has the colour of curd, and forms the source of the great river Mandakini.

तस्याश्रमपदं पुण्यं मृगपक्षिसमन्वितम्।
मेरोः पार्श्वे नगेन्द्रस्य सर्वर्तु कुसुमावृतम्।।99/06।। महा.

स वारुणिस्तपस्तेपे तस्मिन्भरतसत्तम।
वने पुण्यकृतां श्रेष्ठः स्वादु मूलफलोदके।।99/07।।महा.

तस्याश्रमस्योत्तरस्त्रिपुरारिनिषेवितः।
नानारत्नमयैः श्रृंगेः कल्पद्रुमसमन्वितैः।।121/2/1।। म. पु.

मन्दोदकं नाम सरः पयस्तु दधिसन्निभम्।
तस्मात्प्रवहते दिव्या नदी मन्दाकिनी शुभा।।121/2/1-3।। म.पु.

According to *Vayu Purana*, Kailas and Himalayas are the two *mountains* adjoining each other in north and south. They are well-entrenched deep in the ocean on their east and west.

कैलासो हिमवांश्चैव दक्षिणोत्तरपर्वतौ।
पूर्वपश्चायतावेतावर्णवान्तव्यवस्थितौ।।35/9।।

In the *Vishnu Purana*, Kailas and Gandhamadan are stated to be two separate mountains. It says that these two mountains stand extended to east and west, with an expanse of up to 80 *yojanas* (one *yojana* is equal to five miles). Both have their base in the ocean.

गन्धमादनकैलासौ पूर्वपश्चायतावुभौ।।
अशीतियोजनायामर्णवान्तर्व्यवस्थितौ।।2/2/42।।

Going beyond its location, the *Bhagavata Purana* is found highlighting its value, resources, and greatness, stating that the most *beautiful* Mount Kailas is saturated by a variety of precious metals. It becomes golden with the rising sun in the morning.

कैलासशिखरे रम्ये नानाधातुविचित्रिते।
तरुणादित्यसंकाशे तप्तचामीकरप्रभे।।4/6/84/6/8।।

The description of Mount Kailas in ancient literature is such that in terms of prosperity and happiness, there is no place anywhere which could match it even remotely. *Katha Saritsagar* (कथासरित्सागर) refers to the creation of a cave on the peak of the mountain. *Laxminarayan Samhita* (लक्ष्मीधर संहिता) likens it to a mansion, *Kailas Prasad* (कैलास प्रासाद) or *Kailasmeru Prasad* (कैलास-मेरु प्रासाद).

Centre of Mythology and Spirituality

The word "Kailas" in the literal or derivative sense can be interpreted in two ways:

– केलीनां समूहः केलम्, तत्र आस्यते स्थीयते इति कैलासः
(*Kailas means the play ground of Parvati-Shiva*)

– के ब्रह्मणि आस्यते लीयते इति कैलासः
(*Kailas is the place where absolute bliss in its deepest form of meditation or Samadhi is experienced*)

In the Indian philosophical tradition, Kailas is interpreted in various ancient texts in terms of a holy mountain related to (i) divine intelligence or a tutelary deity (आधिदैविक), (ii) elementary or material form (आधिभौतिक) and (iii) spiritual entity (आध्यात्मिक). In this regard, it would be of interest to mention in brief here what has been elaborated with details in the relevant scriptures elsewhere.

From the *Adhidaivik* (आधिदैविक) point of view, Kailas or the *Brahmacharya Kailas* is considered to be the original point of the universe. The *Shiva Purana, Vishveshwar Samhita*

(शिवपुराण, विश्वेश्वरसंहिता) in Chapter 17 states that those who meditate upon Lord Shiva all the while adhering to dharma, truthfulness, and non-violence, are able to cross the cyclic time (काल-चक्र) and the essence of life riding a buffalo. Dharma, symbolized by the bull, rules over the deity who heads the cyclic time, and is akin to or the replica of *Brahmacharya* (ब्रह्मचर्य). Purity, truth, compassion and non-violence are its four legs. Its position is ahead of Shiva Loka (शिवलोक). Its horns are forgiveness. The ears adorned with the chants of the Vedas are the medium for achieving tranquillity. Its two eyes represent piety. Its breath is its pure heart and sharp mind. Dharma in all actions, without interruption, in the form of the bull thus dwells in the Cause or the generating force called Brahma. Shiva who is beyond the cyclic time rides the bull. Every day of Brahma, Vishnu and Maheshwara are their respective lives. There is no day or night beyond that. Birth and death do not exist there.

In a structure of symmetry, with each concentric layer having its own and higher significance, at the base are fourteen *Loka* (worlds) of the Cause or the generating force called Brahma. The five gross elements representing sound, touch, form, fluid and odour do not exist in these 14 Loka of Brahma. They have eternal existence in the form of a subtle odour. Above 14 Loka of Brahma, at the second concentric circle, are 14 Loka of Vishnu, another antecedent force up the ladder. Above them are 28 worlds of Rudra, the third generating force or the Cause. There are 56 Loka of the generating force Shiva above them. The fifth concentric circle above these 56 *Loka is* the ultimate *Brahmacharya Loka*, the beloved world of Shiva. Kailas, the centre of knowledge, covered by the 5 layers is situated there. The sovereign symbol or phallus remain there with 5 charmed circles (पंच-मण्डल), 5 Brahma Kala (ब्रह्म-कला), and the original force (आदि शक्ति). This abode of Lord Shiva, where he lives with his paraashakti (परा शक्ति), is thus described–

अधर्ममहिषारूढं कालचक्रं तरन्ति ते।
सत्यादिधर्मसंयुक्ताः शिवपूजापराश्चये।।84।।

तदूर्ध्वं वृषभो धर्मो ब्रह्मचर्यस्वरूपधृक्।
सत्यादिपादयुक्तस्तु शिवलोकाग्रतः स्थितः।।85।।

क्षमाशृंगः शमः श्रोत्रो वेदध्वनिविभूषितः।
आस्तिक्यचक्षुर्निश्वासः गुरुबुद्धिमनाः वृषः।।86।।

क्रियादिवृषभाज्ञेयाः कारणादिषुसर्वदा।
तं क्रियावृषभं धर्मं कालातीतोऽधितिष्ठति।।87।।

ब्रह्मविष्णुमहेशानां स्वस्वायुर्दिनमुच्यते।
तदूर्ध्वं न दिनं रात्रिर्नजन्ममरणादिकम्।।88।।

पुनः कारणसत्यान्ताः कारणब्रह्मणस्तथा।
गन्धादिभ्यस्तु भूतेभ्यस्तदूर्ध्वं निर्मिताः सदा।।89।।

सूक्ष्मगन्धस्वरूपा हि स्थिता लोकाश्चतुर्दश।
पुनः कारणविष्णोर्वै स्थितालोकाश्चतुर्दश।।90।।

पुनः कारणरुद्रस्य लोकाष्टाविंशका मताः।
पुनश्च कारणेशस्य षट्पंचाशत्तदूर्ध्वगाः।।91।।

ततः परं ब्रह्मचर्यलोकाख्यं शिवसम्मतम्।
तत्रैवज्ञानकैलासे पंचावरणसंयुते।।92।।

पञ्चमण्डलसंयुक्तं पञ्चब्रह्मकलान्वितम्।
आदिशक्तिसमायुक्तमादिलिंगं तु तत्र वै।।93।।

शिवालयमिदं प्रोक्तं शिवस्य परमात्मनः।
परशक्त्या समायुक्तस्तत्रैव परमेश्वर।।94।।

Kurma Purana (कूर्मपुराण–1/4) vividly explains that a water body created at some point of time takes the form of multiple drops. Likewise, a specially-formed water body expands in the form of the universe. The creator is called Brahma (परमेष्ठी) over whom the Ultimate Reality or Brahman presides. He is the original creator and is eternal (सनातन). He is the Soul and is called *Purush* (पुरुष). He exists in the form of a swan (हंस), but is also addressed as *Hiranayagarbh* (हिरण्यगर्भ), *Kapil* (कपिल), and *Chhandamurti* (छन्दमूर्ति). Meru or Kailas is His womb, and various oceans are the fluid in the womb. Mountains are the outer skin of His embryo-

एककालसमुत्पन्नं जलवुद्वुद्वच्च तत्।
विशेषेभ्योऽण्डमभूत्वृहत्तदुदकेशयम्।।36।।

तस्मिन्कार्यस्य करणं संसिद्धिः परमेष्ठिनः।
प्राकृतेऽण्डे विवृत्तः स क्षेत्रज्ञो ब्रह्म संज्ञितः।।37।।

स वै शरीरी प्रथमः स वै पुरुष उच्यते।
आदिकर्ता स भूतानां ब्रह्माग्रे समवर्तत।।38।।

यमाहुः पुरुषं हंसं प्रधानात्परतः स्थितम्।
हिरण्यगर्भं कपिलं छन्दोमूर्तिं सनातनम्।।39।।

मेरुरुल्बमभूत्तस्य जरायुश्चापि पर्वताः।
गर्भोदकं समुद्राश्च तस्यास्य परमात्मनः।।40।।

Similar descriptions exist in *Brahmanda Purana* (ब्रह्माण्ड पुराण1/1/3), *Bhagavata Purana* (भागवत पुराण 5/25) and in many others. Meru or Kailas showing its magnanimous appearance in a triangular or pyramid form is considered to be the centrally-placed womb attracting the entire universe. This is the place where *Hiranyagarbha* (हिरण्यगर्भ) or *Shiva* (शिवतत्त्व) resides. The following mantra of *Rigveda* (ऋग्वेद) is indicative of the universal existence of that supreme, unending Ultimate Reality which has no beginning:

हिरण्यगर्भः समवर्तताग्रे भूतस्य जातः पतिरेक आसीत्।
स दाधार पृथिवीमुत द्यां कस्मै देवाय हविषा विधेम।।

From the material (आधिभौतिक) point of view, the axis binding the North and South Poles of this Earth are called Meru (मेरु). Indeed, the central point of every continent or a major island is called Meru. Kailas, considered to be the centre of spiritual knowledge, in what is known as ancient *Jambudvip* (जम्बूद्वीप), is described as the Meru of the Indian subcontinent called *Bharatavarsha* (भारतवर्ष).

In the *Puranas*, the greater area of Kailas is also described as the centre of "three trees" or *Trivishtapa* (त्रिविष्टप). In depth studies of the *Puranas* clearly suggest that *Trivishtapa* is synonymous with the Greater Himalayas or the *Devabhoomi* (देवभूमि). By the way, in some mythological texts, the other name of Heaven (स्वर्ग) is *Trivishtapa*. With the passage of time, this word got shortened and mutated into '*Tibet*'. The three '*Vitapas*' or trees are considered to be origins of the three mighty rivers, namely, Ganga, Sindhu (Indus) and Brahmaputra. A tree draws water, micro and major nutrients for its survival and grows through hundreds of roots boring into the soil, and uses them to feed hundreds of its branches and thousands of its leaves. Like-wise, a large number of streams, rivulets and tributaries drain their waters into the main stem that forms the river. Before the same river enter an ocean, sea, estuary, lake, or reservoir, it splits into multiple distributaries at its delta. The streams originating from the watershed or catchment area, put together becomes a mighty river, imagery of which is found in the form of a *Vitapa* or tree.

Sindhu (Indus) river, of which the Arabian sea is the destination, is called Vishnu Vitapa. It passes through Kashmir and Ladakh. Laxmi or Vaishno Devi is known to be the wife of Sindhu or Vishnu Vitapa. The land mass considered to be the origin of river Ganga which finally merges in the Indian ocean at Ganga Sagar, is called Shiva Vitapa (matted tresses of Lord Shiva are also called Vitapa). Likewise, the catchment of Brahmaputra river is called Brahma Vitapa. It flows through what is known in the ancient texts as *Brahma Desh* or *Coromandal* (ब्रह्मदेश/कारोमण्दल) before its assimilation into the Bay of Bengal. Here, the words '*Ka*' (क) denotes '*Brahma*' and '*Mandala*' (मण्डल) means 'a specific area'. The river and place of its origin is naturally called *Brahma* Vitapa (ब्रह्मविटप).

One should not miss some amount of symbolism in naming rivers. In the *Purana*, all the major rivers regardless of whether their respective source is in India or not, are named Ganga which underlines their importance and the need to maintain their purity. Kailas region, in terms of its material form (आधिभौतिक रूप) as described in the *Purana* and other ancient texts, has already been discussed briefly in earlier pages.

आध्यात्मिक or spiritual aspect of Kailas is the most serious one. Proper understanding and internalization of this aspect is possible only for a most evolved yogi pursuing the path of spirituality who has experienced the Ultimate Reality within himself. The spiritual interpretation of Kailas here is only indicative from a layman's point of view.

It is thus stated in spiritual texts that our body itself in the abode of Ultimate Reality called God- "शरीरं देवमन्दिरम्". The intensity of the relationship or coordination between the left and right halves of the brain determine human intelligence. A higher degree of intensity or intimate relationship between the two sides of the brain lead to sharper intelligence, specially in the spiritual sense. At the centre is the meeting place of the three *Nadis* or special arteries called Ida (इड़ा), *Pingala*

(पिंगला) and *Sushumna* (सुषुम्ना). In the yogic language these nadis are also called Ganga, Yamuna and Saraswati, respectively. Just above the *Agya Chakra* (आज्ञाचक्र), the third eye (*chakra)* or the sixth primary *chakra* where these three *Nadis* meet is called '*Trikut*' (त्रिकूट) which is the other name of Kailas (कैलास).

The intense relationship between the left and right halves of the brain is the exchange of words between Shiva and Parvati. That is the source of eternal knowledge. In his famous book '*Saundarya Lahari*' (सौन्दर्यलहरी) containing secrets of mysticism in symbolic form, Adi Sankara seems to have given some hints using the term "swans" by stating–

समुन्मीलत्संवित्कमलमकरन्दैकरसिकं
भजे हंसद्वन्द्वं किमपि महतां मानसचरम्।
यदालापादष्टादशगुणितविद्या परिणतिः।
यदादत्ते दोषाद्गुणमखिलमद्भ्यः पय इव।।38।।

(I sing the song of the pair of swans who are the only ones to enjoy the honey of the lotus that blossoms in the heart of great souls and who undertake pleasure walks in their mind called Manasarovar. The interaction between the pair of swans results in the revelation of 18 branches of knowledge. This pair of swans extracts the truth from illusion like milk from milk mixed in water.)

The famous mantra of *Mundak Upanishad* below highlights the vital truth similarly through another parable-

द्वासुपर्णा सयुजा सखाया समानं वृक्षं परिषस्व जाते।
तयोरन्यः पिप्पलं स्वाद्वत्ति अनश्नन्नन्यो अभिचाकशीति।।3/1/।।

(Two friendly birds occupy the same tree. One of them eats seeds but the other one remains a mere spectator.)

Another parable explains the same point stating, "*In the centre of* Sushumna, *there are two Matsyas (मत्स्य; fish) between the two Nadis in the form of Ganga and Yamuna. The consumer (controller) of these two fish is called the seeker (साधक) of fish."* That is, "inhalation" and "exhalation" of breath are the two fish in two Nadis– *Ida* and *Pingala* (Ganga and Yamuna). The two fish are controlled or suspended by the seeker through breath-control or *Pranayam* (प्राणायाम). In that condition, life force flows upwards in *Sushumna*-

गंगायमुनायोर्मध्ये मत्स्यौ द्वौ चरतः सदा।
तौ मत्स्यौ भक्षयेद्यस्तु स भवेन्मत्स्यसाधकः।।

As the principal source of knowledge in the tradition of spirituality, Shiva is also depicted in the form of a banyan tree. Aerial prop-roots of the banyan tree drop down to the ground and grow over time becoming indistinguishable from the main trunk of the tree. Likewise, the Guru upon whom the *Shiva tattva* stands revealed, imparts divine knowledge to transform his worthy disciple and makes him like himself. The imagery of the banyan tree on the shores of Manasarovar where Kuber used to spent some time after taking dips in the lake is symbolic and suggestive of the spiritual truth in the narrative.

Kailas evokes poetry

Kailas' description through the poetry of the great creative genius Kalidas is being provided herewith to give a fleeting flavour of the literary world it touched. In the famous book *Meghadutam* of the Sanskrit poet Kalidas, Yaksha in exile at a far-off place in Ramagiri hills in central India pines for his beloved wife leading a lonely life in Alaka Puri to the north of Kailas. He gives the following advice to the Cloud, his messenger-

हित्वा तस्मिन्भुजगवलयं शम्भुनादत्तहस्ता
क्रीडाशैले यदि च विचरेत्पादचारेण गौरी।

भंगी भक्त्या विरचितवपुः स्तम्भितान्तर्जलौघः
सोपानत्वं कुरु मणितटारोहणायाग्रयायी।।

(O Cloud! In Kailas, which is the playground of the couple, Lord Shiva-Parvati, you may see Gauri taking a walk holding the hand of her lover adorned with a bracelet of snakes. You should appear before her humbly and respectfully transforming yourself into a solid form to be used as stairs by her for climbing onto her throne decorated with a variety of jewels on top of the mountain')

The Yaksha warns the Cloud messenger not to get distracted by the scenes that may unfold before him:

तत्रावश्यं वलयकुलिशोद्धट्टनोद्गीर्णतोयं
नेष्यन्ति त्वां सुरयुवतयो यन्त्रधारागृहत्वम्।
ताभ्यो मोक्षस्तव यदि सखे घर्मलब्धस्य न स्यात्
क्रीडालोलाश्रवणपरुषैर्गर्जितैर्भाययेथा।।

(The celestial maidens in this entertainment ground of Shiva-Parvati, namely, Kailas, may indulge in play by assembling below and using you as a shower instrument to get relief from perspiration due to their exposure to the hot sunlight. If they try hitting you with their hands beautifully adorned with bracelets embellished with jewels and gem stones, scare them by growling and move ahead towards your task without getting distracted.)

Kailas, surrounded by mountains on all four sides, evokes thoughts of Lord Shiva sitting in a meditative posture on a lotus and being adorned by petals from all four sides. It also seems as if the surrounding mountains from all sides are offering their holy oblations to Kailas which has the look and feel of a pagoda due to its dome-shape and because it happens to be the home of Lord Shiva. These mountains too seem to want to experience bliss by performing the rituals and paying obeisance to the presiding deity. Through two vertical peaks, water from snow-capped Kailas reaches the partly-frozen rich emerald green Gauri Kund.

Mount Kailas as described in ancient literature, including mythological texts, has a variety of flora and fauna. There are different types of plants, flowers, fruit-bearing trees, creepers, and vines in this garden of Lord Shiva which is also frequented by other divine creatures and sages. Flowers which blossom in different seasons are found blooming in Kailas round-the-year which keep this place perpetually beautiful. Celestial maidens in neighbouring Alaka Puri decorate themselves gorgeously using beautiful fresh flowers that grow in the place round the year.

Poet Kalidas in *Meghadutam* has conveyed this poetic truth describing the appearance of these celestial maidens attractively and seductively–

हस्ते लीलाकमलमलके बालकुन्दानुविद्धं
नीता लोध्रप्रसवरजसा पाण्डुतामानने श्री।
चूड़ापाशे नवकुरवकं चारुकर्णे शिरीषं
सीमन्ते च त्वदुपगमजं यत्र नीपं वधूनाम्।।

(Brides in Alaka Puri decorate themselves holding lotus flowers in their hands, jasmine (कुन्द) in their hair, tendrils of cinchona (लोध्र, symplocos racemose) curl on their face, fresh crimson amaranth flowers (कुरवक) adorn their dressed hair, with blue jacaranda (शिरीष) their ears, and orange flowers of cadamba (कदम्ब, burr-flower tree) the central parting of hair above the forehead.)

[Flowers that bloom in all six seasons usually associated with India have been referred to – the lotus blooms in autumn; jasmine in hemant (pre-winter); cinchona in winter;

amaranth in spring; jacaranda in summer; and cadamba in rainy season.]

Notwithstanding the contradictions between poetic licence and ground reality as we notice currently, it may not be illogical to assign some of the paradoxes to geographical changes that might have taken place in the course of time. There might be a pre-glacial period when the greater Himalayas had an ocean towards its east and west as has been hinted by Kalidas in his epic *Kumarasambhavam* and also in *Pauranic* texts. The Tibetan plateau is also known as a frozen desert. Many geo-scientists believe that it was uplifted from the ocean as a result of collision of the tectonic plates over 50 million years ago. Besides geology, there is also hardly any contradiction in the description of supernatural phenomenon pertaining to the Himalayas, and particularly to Mount Kailas and Manasarovar, for the accomplished yogis and seekers. For them, divinity simply can not be experienced by gross eyes or senses.

Mount Kailas in other forms

In the land described in ancient texts as the home and playground of Lord Shiva and his family, what is visible, perceived and cognizable to the gross senses of ordinary pilgrims is a snow-capped unusual mountain in the shape of a dome surrounded by a number of somewhat lower peaks containing naked rocks and stones and valleys. There is hardly any vegetative growth, much less flowers of different seasons blooming round the year. On the lower slopes below perma-frost, a few creeping plants and sparce thorny bushes of dama plant, similar to juniper or European gorse, 2 to 3 feet high, can be found, which the local population use to light fires. The wider mountain region is characterized by a shallow soil cover, on which only perennial frost-resistant plants grow with roots reaching the bedrock.

Yet the place continues to hypnotize and emit divinity, its environment spiritually vibrant and energizing. Followers of different faiths since aeons have remained eager in perpetuity to have a glimpse of their treasured Mount Kailas. The magnetic effect of holy Kailas is all pervasive, all the time. This unique most-revered mountain, but perhaps least visited due to its inaccessibility and remoteness, created by the divine architect has no temples around. Indeed, it itself appears in the shape of a naturally-built grand temple beautified in silver-white colour by the never-melting snow, becoming golden during sunrise and multi-hued during sunset. Its appeal is universal, undiminished. For the devotees of Bholenath, Mount Kailas remains matchless, the ultimate destination. Sages and seers continue to visit this sacred place quietly to achieve enlightenment and to experience absolute bliss. It is believed that many accomplished yogis who do not like to be seen, still inhabit places around Mount Kailas.

There is an interesting tale in the *Aranyaka Parva* (आरण्यक पर्व) of *Mahabharata*. When the great Vaivasvat Manu was in deep meditation in *Badarikashram*, a fish from river Virani (वीरणी) sought his shelter. The King obliged her by providing a pond to live in. After getting the shelter, the fish started growing very fast. As it was not possible for the pond to accommodate the ever-growing fish, Vaivasvat Manu was left with no option but to release her in the ocean. At that time the grateful fish told the sage king that with the passage of time when the entire earth starts sinking in the sea, he should board a boat and recall her. As predicted by the fish, places around the Himalayas started sinking, and recalling the offer from the fish, Vaivasvat Manu collected a variety of seeds to protect the creation of almighty and boarded a boat along with the seven sages:

बीजान्यादाय सर्वाणि सागरं पुप्लुवे तदा।
नावा तु शुभया वीर महोर्मिणमरिन्दम।।

On being approached, the fish had appeared before the sage king and offered the desired protection. The boat was tied in the horn of the fish which was steered to the highest peak of the Himalayas known as Gobandhan. The boat was tethered there:

अस्मिन्हिमवतः शृंगे नावं बन्धीत माचिरम्।
साबद्धास्तत्र तैस्तूर्णमृषिभिर्भरतर्षभ।।

The narrative seems to suggest that places with snow-covered mountains today were witnessing oceanic waves during an unknown period of history. Nevertheless, the holiness and importance of *tirthas* do not suffer anyway even if their geographical features as depicted in ancient literature, fail to pass the tests of modern times. It is in keeping with tradition, that supernatural phenomenon is sometimes symbolic in conveying the non-obvious spiritual and metaphysical meanings. Rightly said– "कलौ नामानि पूज्यन्ते" or 'कलियुग केवल नाम अधारा' (*In Kali Yuga, reciting the names of the Lord matters*). A forest of basil plants (वृन्दावन) was the place of entertainment for Krishna and Gopis in the distant past. It continues to remain a holy place for Hindus even though the physical features of the place as described in age-old texts do not exist. Archaeological research and discovery of artifacts suggests that the Tibetan plateau did have a vegetative cover in a pre-glacial age.

Devotees of Shiva try to see images of various Gods, Goddesses and other divine beings in the rocks and stones of various shapes and sizes found in the mountain ranges that surround Mount Kailas. It is not easy to correlate the visible mountains with those mentioned in mythological texts. *Gandhamadan* (गन्धमादन), the place of life-saving medicine Sanjivani (संजीवनी), *Suryaprabha* (सूर्यप्रभ), *Chandraprabha* (चंद्रप्रभ), etc. are mountains in the vicinity of Mount Kailas described in the *Purana*. The peaceful environment of Mount Kailas strengthens this faith of devotee-pilgrims that there could not have been a more appropriate place for the Greatest Yogi (Shiva) who swallowed the poison that came out as a result of churning of the ocean and secured it by storing it in his throat.

Mount Kailas is the place which tells the importance of austerity and sacrifice in the process of evolution to achieve the highest goal of life. It does not represent civilization as it is understood today in terms of material products displayed for conspicuous consumption. Mount Kailas flags off peace and harmony to be the tools in realizing the true potential of human beings and to go beyond the non-obvious. It is only for this reason that the greatest sages and yogis chose this holy place to pursue their goal of experiencing the Ultimate Reality within oneself by ignoring the creature comforts of material life, voluntarily. *Pushpadanta*, the King of *Gandharva* and a great devotee of Lord Shiva, rightly described metaphorically the attributes of his beloved deity who remained detached in the solitude-

श्मशानेष्वाक्रीडा स्मरहरपिशाचाः सहचाराः
चिताभस्मालेपः सृगपिनृकरोटी परिकरः।
अमंगल्यं शीलं तव भवतु नामैवमखिलं
तथापि स्मर्तृणां वरद परमं मंगलमसि।।

(He plays in the cremation ground, ghosts and vampires are his companions; He smears the ashes of the burnt bodies of the dead on his body, wears a garland of human skulls around his neck, and appears as though inauspicious and in terrifying form. But, in spite of being the controller of cravings, he offers everything auspicious and takes care of those who remember him in devotion.)

The Greatest among all Yogis, whose only asset is an old bull called Nandi, is called the Lord of all Gods or the *Maheshvara* even though he lives in complete solitude at Mount Kailas. As the legend goes, the King of Demons, Ravana, had acquired unlimited powers by pleasing the principal deity of Kailas, Lord Shiva, through penance and meditation. He had captured all the valuable assets from Gods in heaven including the *Pushpak Viman*, air chariot of Kuber. Completely filled with unmatched arrogance about his unlimited powers, when he tried to unsettle Mount Kailas, the abode of Shiva, what happened is narrated by Pushpadanta as follows:

अमुष्य त्वत्सेवासमधिगतसारं भुजवनं
बलात्कैलासेऽपि त्वधिवसतौ विक्रमयतः।
अलभ्या पातालेऽप्यलसचलितांगुष्ठशिरसि
प्रतिष्ठात्वय्यासीत्धुव्र मुपचितो मुह्यति खलः।।

(Ravana tried to use his powerful hands, which had once upon a time served you to be blessed, for uprooting Mount Kailas in spite of knowing that it is your home. He had to suffer ignominy by being crushed and pushed into the nether world when Lord Shiva just touched the mountain with the tip of his toe. It is often the case that an evil-minded creature intoxicated with the arrogance of power forgets his very benefactor.)

It is the detached life of this Greatest Yogi of Kailas that made one and all his admirers which included Lord Vishnu. *Pushpadanta* recalls a compelling episode in this regard. Lord Vishnu, who is also known as the Lotus-Eyed God, used to offer prayers at the feet of Lord Shiva with punctuality everyday with one thousand lotus flowers. Suddenly once when he found that there was shortage of one, he plucked out one of his own eyes and offered it in place of the missing lotus flower-

हरिस्ते साहस्रं कमलबलिमाधाय पदयोः
यदेकोने नित्यं निजमुदहरन्नेत्रकमलम्।

Lord Shiva is famous for his magnanimous nature and kindness. He melts and pardons when finds his devotees in pain. Ravana was crushed and pushed into hell when he tried to indulge in the misadventure of unsettling Mount Kailas. But he was not only rescued when he started crying in pain at being crushed under the weight of the same mountain when pressed down with the tip of Shiva's toe, but also given a warm send-off by the supreme deity of Kailas with the gift of his sword *Chandrahas*. The great poet Kalidas also referred to this misadventure of Ravana when he praises the greatness and divinity of Kailas metaphorically. The main protagonist *Yaksha* in his book *Meghadutam* guides and advises his Cloud messenger as to how he should conduct himself when he reaches Kailas on the way to Alaka Puri as follows-

गत्वा चोर्ध्वं दशमुखभुजोच्छ्वासितप्रस्थस्कन्धे
कैलासस्य त्रिदशवनितादर्पणस्यातिथिः स्याः।
श्रंगोच्छायैः कुमुदविततैर्योवितत्य स्थितः खं
राशीभूतः प्रतिदिनमिव त्र्यम्बकस्याट्टहासः।

(O Cloud! after proceeding in the northerly direction crossing many mountains and valleys, you would reach Mount Kailas whose base had been shaken by Ravana using his all-powerful hands. You must accept the hospitality of this snow-capped mountain whose slopes have a bright lustre which is used by the heavenly maidens as though a polished mirror. Kailas appears like a white lotus flower in full bloom kissing the sky. Glancing from a distance, it appears as if with a loud all-knowing laugh the three-eyed Shiva has taken a solid form.)

Naked raw mountains all around it do not undermine the everlasting natural beauty of the sparkling Kailas. On the contrary, their varied shapes and locations with reference to Kailas evoke the images of his family members and others like Nandi, his bull-ride, and embed a deeper faith among the devotees of Lord Shiva. Depending upon their perceptions, devotees start imagining their own creations. They also arouse curiosity bordering on wonder among non-believers as well, with photographs and commentary on Kailas and the interesting associations of surrounding mountains with various mythological characters dotting the internet-web pages in large numbers. The famous Swedish geographer Dr. Sven Hedin was spot on when he wrote, '*It is incomparably the most famous mountain in the World. Mount Everest and Mount Blanc cannot vie with it*'.

In the *Mahabharata*, there are descriptions of the *Kinnara,* people who exhibit a rude nature particularly in their behaviour and dealings with others. It is not rare to find such people even today. Indeed, a few of those who pretend to offer services of yaks, ponies and porters may remind the pilgrims of such descriptions made in the great epic. But then, this is hardly unusual. Various religious places and symbols have been misused by bad elements in every era. After all, the demon king Ravana came to kidnap Mother Sita in a saffron robe presenting himself as a monk!

It is an irony of our times that many of us visit Kailas, the abode of a detached and penniless God, to seek wealth and material prosperity from him rather than strength to get detached from material possessions one by one in order to be happy. The difficult route of parikrama of Mount Kailas by seekers of spirituality now-a-days is crowded with craving for worldly comforts. Even so, even today some true devotees of Lord Shiva continue to take solace in trekking around

Mount Kailas and drinking the milky waters of streams originating from its peak.

Kailas is Ultimate in Bon, Buddhism and Jainism

Bon faith (a tribal faith that predates Tibetan Buddhism), Buddhism and Jainism too associate the highest sacredness to Mount Kailas.

Much of the research on the Bon religion starts with the work done by Prof. David L. Snellgrove in close association with a knowledgeable representative of the Bon religion, Lopon Tenzin Namdak, and published in *The Nine Ways* of Bon. Accordingly, the Bonpas, followers of Bon religion, maintain that their religion has universal traits and define it as the Eternal or Everlasting Bon. The founder of this Everlasting Bon is the Teacher *gShen-rab Mi-bo-che*, who appeared before the historical Buddha, lived and spread his teachings from a land to the West of Tibet called *sTaggzig*. What we can observe of Bon religion today is a tradition that came to be organized as of the tenth or eleventh century AD following the decay of the Tibetan empire. This religious tradition does not acknowledge the shamanistic Indian origin of its doctrines and practices.

Professor Per Kvaerne of University of Oslo in his specialization on the Bon religion marks a first attempt to describe the Bonpo iconography in a systematic way. He presents a selection of paintings and statues, mostly from Tibet, of major deities and spiritual figures and describes them in terms of form and content as well as through translated excerpts, including mythological ones. He shows that the Bonpo version of the 'Wheel of Existence' - the circle of transmigration of sentient beings - assimilates elements which are present in Tibetan culture as a whole, while retaining a considerable degree of freedom in utilising these elements according to its own religious concepts.

Thus, the Bon religion is still followed today in Tibet and in Tibetan-inhabited areas of India and Nepal. Although Bon may appear quite similar to Buddhism in some respects, there are in fact definite differences. To some of the Bon followers, Kailas is the left-facing "Nine-storeyed Swastika Mountain" and the mystic soul of the entire region. They call it Tise and believe it to be seat of the Sky Goddess Sipaimen. The union of Mount Kailas and Lake Manasarovar marks a holy site for the Bonpo, the two being "the mother and father of the earth". To some others, the foremost symbol is the *Vajra,* the indestructible and eternal. The Bonpo perform the kora in the anti-clockwise direction.

In the Buddhist system, Kailas is Kang Rinpoche (Precious One of Glacial Snow). Though historically, Buddhism entered Tibet in the seventh century AD, the Buddha is said to have magically visited Kailas in the fifth century BC. According to Tibetan mythology, Mount Kailas is the centre of the universe. In Kanagari Karchhak (Tibetan Kailas Purana), it is stated that there is a wish-granting divine tree on one side of Mount Kailas. The square-shaped area adjoining this mountain is saturated with golden jewels. The eastern face of Mount Kailas contains crystal gems, the southern side blue sapphire, and the northern side gold. The mountain is stated to be covered by variety of fragrant flowers and medicinal plants from all sides.

With Kailas at the centre, four gompas or temples were built at the four cardinal points, and four prostration points indicate four directions. The foot-imprint of the Buddha is to be found all over Western Tibet, but four of these have special significance and are found adorning prominent rocks on all four sides of Mount Kailas during the outer kora. Legends abound that it is due to these foot-prints that Gods are unable to lift Mount Kailas to their heaven. It is also said to be held tightly by chains from all four sides so that those below the mountain are unable to pull it down towards them either. Tibetan literature also speaks of four rivers arising from the world mountain– north-flowing Senge Khambab from the Mouth of the Lion (river Indus); east-flowing Dachok Khambab with its face of crystal from the Horse Mouth (river Brahmaputra/ Tsangpo); south-flowing Mapcha Khambab with its face of Lapis Lazuli from the Mouth of the Peacock (river Karnali); and west-flowing Langchen Khambab with its face of ruby from the Elephant Mouth (river Sutlej). In Buddhist texts, Mount Kailas is believed to be the legendary Mount Meru, the centre of Buddhist cosmology, which reaches from the lowest hell to the highest heaven. Tantric Buddhists believe that it is the home of Buddha Demchok representing supreme bliss.

A famous legend relates to the contest for control of Kailas between Karma Kagyu school in Tibetan Buddhism, which was fought by Milarepa, the legendary guru, yogi and poet of the eleventh century, and Bon faith led by Naro Bönchung, their priest and champion. For days the two wise monks had engaged in a ferocious battle of magic, but neither had been able to gain the upper hand, so well-matched were they. It was agreed to settle the matter in a final, winner-takes-all magical duel, which would be a straightforward race to the top of Mount Kailas. Naro Boen-Chung instantly mounted his magic drum and started to soar up the slope of the mountain. Unperturbed by the progress made by his rival, Milarepa merely sat down to meditate. But rising at dawn, he was carried by a ray of sunlight directly to the summit. Shocked by this feat and Milarepa's victory, Naro Bönchung tumbled off his drum, which skittered down the south face of the mountain, gouging the long slash marking Mount Kailas to this day. The legend continues that gracious in victory, Milarepa decreed that Bön followers could continue to make their customary anti-clockwise circuits of the holy Kailas, and throwing a handful of snow onto the nearby peak of Mount Bönri, bequeathed it forever to the Bonpas their own holy mountain. These actions despite clear victory helped to maintain in the connections of both faiths to the sacred region of Kailas.

The presiding meditational deity of Mount Kailas, Demchok (*Chakrasamvara)* is stated to wear the skin of lion and a garland of human skulls besides holding a trident in one hand and pellet drum (डमरु) in the other. Dorje Phangmo (*Vajra-Varahi,* when in wrathful form*)*, his spouse, remains in the arms with her husband all the time. Together the pair symbolizes the mystic duality of compassion and wisdom which result in spiritual Enlightenment. In the western direction of Kailas, there is a mountain named Taijung which is covered by snow all the time. This mountain is known to be the original place of Dorje Phagmo. It is further said that Gods reside around Kailas in 990 rows. All of them wear tiger skin. Lord Buddha is also stated to reside on the peak of Kailas along with his 500 Bodhisattvas, enlightened beings who have chosen to stay there to help others attain Nirvana. Three hills around Kang Rinpoche are said to be the abodes of Bodhisattvas, Manjushri, Vajrapani, and Avalokitesvara. The king of monkeys is said to live at the foot of Mount Kailas. It is believed that only the rarest of the rare with pure hearts are privileged to meet the Gods and Goddesses of Kailas. Melodious sounds of various musical instrument are also heard in Kailas according the Tibetan mythological descriptions.

After reading these tales, it is not difficult to imagine the confluence of Indian and Tibetan mythological texts. For the tradition-bound conservative Tibetans, Kang Rinpoche is the most holy place they remain eager to visit. Like the

Kumbha Festival in India celebrated with vigour after a gap of certain number of years, Tibetans too celebrate a similar festival in Mount Kailas. From the lamas to the common man, specially those from Purang valley, all wait eagerly to participate in this important festival in the Horse Year.

Jain scriptures have singled out five central events (*Pancha Kalyanak*) that occur in a Tirthankara's lifetime as most auspicious moments. The first event is the descent of a Tirthankara into the mother's womb signified by her having 14 auspicious dreams. The second is his actual birth which is celebrated with great splendour. The third is renunciation of all riches and wealth and start of the arduous and long ascetic life. After deep contemplation and meditation, he attains omniscience (*Keval-Jnan*). The last event is *Nirvana Kalyanak* when his soul is finally freed from all karmic bonds and is liberated to attain *Siddhi*. *Nirvana-bhoomi* or five key pilgrimages (*Maha Tirthas)* where all 24 Tirthankaras attained Nirvana are: Adinath Bhagwan Rishabhadev at Ashtapad, Mahavir Swami at Pavapuri, Vasupujya Swami at Champäpuri, and Bhagwan Neminath at Girnar. The other 20 Tirthankaras attained Nirvana at Samet Shikhar.

The followers of Jainism address Kailas by the name Ashtapad (अष्टपद), and consider it to be among their holiest shrines. They believe that it is their pious duty to visit it. The ancient Jain literature, in *Uttaradhyayan Sutra Niryukti*, says that anyone (*Charam Shariri*) who can scale Ashtapad Tirth will attain Nirvana or Moksha, and describes the Kailas as a 'Mountain of Gold and Silver'. Ashtapad literally means eight steps which could be either eight giant steps to ascend the mountain or a chain of eight mountain peaks. The Ekadash Angadi Ägam, the oldest text, mentions Ashtapad as a Maha-Tirth. Manasarovar has been described as *Padma Hrada* (पद्महृद) in ancient Jain literature.

Legend as mentioned in *Sutra Krutänga Sutra* has it that Chakravarti King Bharat (son of Bhagwan Shri Rishabhadev) had built a palace with precious stones at this place as a memorial to commemorate the Nirvana of Bhagwan Rishabhadev. With regard to Ashtäpad, it describes certain details about the Tirthankaras. It is said that once after attaining absolute knowledge, Bhagwan Rishabhadev was delivering a sermon while seated in *Samavasaran*. Out of curiosity, King Bharat asked if any human being present here would become a Tirthankara in the future. He replied affirmatively and said his son *Marichi* will become the 24th Tirthankar after many life cycles and will be known as *Mahavir*. He subsequently explained the upcoming *Chovisi* (24 Tirthankaras). This is how King Bharat came to know details of present *Chovisi*. It is said that Bhagwan Mahavir once said during his sermon that any human being, who can scale this mountain and stay overnight there, will attain liberation in his life time.

Presence of sages in Kailas-Manasarovar Region

In the ancient texts, there are large number of references and tales of sages and accomplished yogis inhabiting caves and valleys of the Himalayas and some of the most evolved ones among them pursuing deeper forms of meditation in and around Kailas-Manasarovar. Far from the madding crowd, these seekers wanted to demystify the non-obvious universe and unravel the secrets of life through their experience-based experimentations.

Public curiosity about the great souls residing in the most inhospitable conditions of Kailas-Manasarovar region continues till date. Many yogis in the twentieth century have written books mentioning vivid details of how they were initiated and taught by sages and yogis residing in Himalayan caves, including in Kailas-Manasarovar region. Swami

Pranavanandji lived in Gompas situated on the shores of Manasarovar for a long time and found most of the assumptions in relation to the existence of great yogis and saints exaggerative. Nevertheless, on the basis of his personal experiences, he found the environment of Kailas-Manasarovar spiritually charged though this might not be experienced by every visitor.

There are legends and tales suggestive of the existence of caves inside Mount Kailas which do not come to the sight of gross eyes of pilgrims. These caves are where the immortal sages and yogis in control of their lives are said to reside. The great yogi Paramahansa Vishuddhanandji learnt the finer aspects of yoga and solar science from his teachers in Tibet's Kailas-Manasarovar region as recorded by some of his great disciples and scholars including Mahamahopadhya late Gopinath Kaviraj.

One of the greatest yogis of the twentieth century, Paramahansa Vishuddhanandaji demonstrated his knowledge of solar science before renowned physicists by producing odours of flowers that bloomed in different seasons and different regions including in Tibet. For him, his expertise in using special type of lenses and Sun's rays in a particular manner was not a miracle. He could bring life to dead creatures although would do this sparingly to prove that Sun is the source of energy that sustains life on earth. He wanted to promote techniques of solar science which had been taught to him by his teachers at a centre of learning in Kailas-Manasarovar region for many years, but could not do so in the absence of requisite materials for his laboratory which he tried to establish in Varanasi.

Swami Ram in his book "*Living with Himalayan Masters*" refers to his grandmaster who lived in a cave in Kailas. He acquired the yogic expertise for converting matter into energy and vice versa from this great yogi on the direction of his master who had initiated him to yoga. In the yogic tradition and literature, details of such expertise are strictly prohibited to be shared in public. Patanjali in Yoga-sutras explains how the accomplished yogis have nothing inaccessible and how they can go beyond sight in super natural bodies. There are methods hinted in the Yoga-sutras to get unaffected by hunger, thirst and vagaries of weather. Yogis are prohibited from demonstrating powers of their accomplishments as such things obstruct in achieving *Samadhi* (ते समाधौ उपसर्गा व्युत्थाने सिद्धय:). Swami Pranavanand has himself stated that the spiritual vibrations felt by seekers and yogis may not be felt by others.

In some old scriptures, it is mentioned that the son of Lord Shiva pierced the *Kraunch* mountain with his powerful arrows once when he got angry. This mountain is said to be in the vicinity of Mount Kailas. Probably this son of Lord Shiva and Goddess Parvati is known as *Sanagpa* in the Tibetan mythological texts. "*Lha Chhu*" river that flows in the west of Kailas is the second mother of Sanagpa according to local legends. Similarly, Demchok, the presiding deity of Kailas, is said to be his father. The river Ganga is described as the river of Gods. Likewise, the river *Lha Chhu* is called the river of Gods. "*Lha*" in the local language means God and "*Chhu*" means water. *Lha Chhu* can be said to be the other name of Ganga which first alighted on the head of Lord Shiva, and remained for a considerable period wandering among the tresses of his long and entangled hair, before springing out and falling on the earth's surface.

As stated earlier, the similarity between Indian and Tibetan mythological episodes cannot be lost sight of. *Chiu Gompa* by the side of river *Lha Chhu* is famous for the being the residence of sages. Local people with faith in the tradition believe even today that there are many Gompas where Gods live as guests of *Sanagpa* and protect their animals, the main source of subsistence for them.

According to another legend, long time back a highly learned lama named *Nyen* had come to Lha Chhu valley and constructed a monastery there. It is said that the highly-evolved Nyen lama possessed divine powers. He appeared as though he was energy personified. His face sparkled, as if emitting fire. He constructed the monastery as per the directions of *Sanagpa*. It is said that inside this monastery, which was located very close to *Sanagpa's* mansion, *Nyen* lama installed an idol of Buddha in the form of Amitabh. It is a matter of inference whether *Nyen* lama was the other name of sage *Angira* who is a personification of fire in Hindu scriptures. Sage Angira and sage Sanat Kumar had studied together in Kailas, according to Hindu scriptures.

The Hindu scriptures contain many narratives to explain the association of great many sages and warriors with Mount Kailas and Lord Shiva. It is said that *Parashu Rama* acquired his incomparable expertise in archery from Lord Shiva in Kailas. In competing with Kartikeya, the son of Lord Shiva, *Parashu Rama* is stated to have pierced *Kraunch* mountain near Kailas by the force of his arrow to demonstrate his archery skill. He is reported to have exited from Kailas through a large hole thus created in this mountain. Legends say that after returning from Kailas, *Parashu Rama* had killed the *Kshatriya* kings 21 times when he found them indulging in activities which went against their own subjects. In *Meghadutam* of Kalidas, there is a reference indicating the access point for Kailas through the hole created by sage-warrior *Parashu Rama*. *Yaksha* advises his Cloud-messenger that he should enter Kailas and Alaka Puri through this entrance or access point created by *Parashu Rama*. He underlines the importance of this access point through which the royal swans of Manasarovar go back to their home after spending winter season in the hospitable plains in India:

प्रालेयाद्रेरुपतटमतिक्रम्य तास्तान्विशेषान्
हंसद्वारं भृगुपतियशोवर्त्मयत्क्रौंचरंध्रम्।
तेनोदीचिं दिशिमनुसरेत्तिर्यगायामशोभी
श्यामः पादो वलिनियमनाभ्युद्यतस्येव विष्णोः।।

(Having passed upon various objects of curiosity near the skirt of Himalaya proceed to the north, looking beautiful by your length extended crosswise like the dark foot of Vishnu when ready to put down Bali, by the opening in mount Krauncha, the gate of swans and the very path of glory of the most eminent of the Parashu Rama.)

In the Vana *Parva* (वनपर्व) of *Mahabharata*, it is stated to Yudhishthira that it is after crossing Mount Kailas that the greatest sages are found radiating enlightenment:

अस्यातिक्रम्य शिखरं कैलासस्य युधिष्ठिरः।
गतिः परमसिद्धानां देवर्षीणां प्रकाशते।।

In order to further satiate his curiosity, sage Arshtishen (आर्ष्टिषेण) tells, '*O great Yudhishthira! at the time of oneness between full moon and moonlessness, many sages come flying through the sky in this superior-most mountain of Kailas for their best moments. Some sustain life only on air and many others on water. It is not possible to proceed further. Beyond this is the place of Gods which is inaccessible to human beings*':

न चाप्यतः परं शक्यं गन्तुं भरतसत्तम।
विहारो ह्यत्र देवानाममानुषगतिस्तु सा।।

The great sage-scholar Patanjali in his Yoga-sutras speaks of accomplishments through yogic practices, which are considered supernatural. Thus, a yogi can expand his body to his desire, or shrink it to a size small enough to penetrate anything. He can fly like a bird by making his body extremely light, and also get inside solid forms like rocks. Patanjali has warned the seekers that public demonstration of such accomplishments becomes a hindrance in achieving further progress to reach the highest level of enlightenment. Exhibition of accomplishments for livelihood or fame after achieving partial success in the yogic practices is thus disapproved by Patanjali and in sacred books. Such exhibition has serious adverse consequences for the yoga school of metaphysics, says Swami Shivananda, a great yogi and scholar of modern India.

The great yogis are also unconcerned about earning name or fame. Nor are they attracted to worldly comforts manifest in raising a family and amassing wealth. Detached from social recognition and similar paraphernalia, they spent time incognito to enjoy the bliss achieved by realizing oneness with the Ultimate Reality in solitude and in the remoteness of Himalayan caves. It is possible that highly evolved sages, reluctant to be revealed, do reside in caves and monasteries in and around Kailas-Manasarovar or transformed in forms invisible to unaccomplished people. It is said that they shun public glare nor share their knowledge of theosophy (ब्रह्मविद्या) with those who lack requisite absorptive capacity. Says the great Manu emphatically, '*let the knower of Brahma Vidya die with his knowledge without it being shared with others. He must not impart it to those who are not eligible, even at the cost of his life*':

विद्ययैव मृतं कामं मर्तव्यं ब्रह्मवादिना।
आपत्स्वपि हि घोरायां न त्वेनामिरिणे वपेत्।।

It is also possible that even after meeting them, one fails to recognize the highly accomplished yogis for their true worth. Our naked eyes and senses are hardly capable of grasping the non-obvious or internalising something extraordinary. It was not possible even for Arjun, a seeker of very high order, to see Lord Krishna in his supernatural form. He was granted divine vision by his Master to see and experience the omniscience, omnipresence and omnipotence in his Charioteer, Lord Krishna:

न तु मां शक्यसे द्रष्टुमनेनैव स्वचक्षुसा
दिव्यं ददामि ते चक्षुः पश्य मे योगमश्वरम्।।

On several occasions, Lord Krishna reminds Arjuna in the Gita that it is extremely difficult to experience the Ultimate Reality called *Brahman*. A seeker remaining in quest of knowledge continuously for many austere lives only is able to see Him at the end, says Lord Krishna:

अनेकजन्मसंसिद्धस्ततो याति परां गतिम्।
बहूनां जन्मनामन्ते ज्ञानवान्मां प्रपद्यते।।

Likewise meeting accomplished sages who after self-realization experience oneness with the Ultimate Reality could not be easy and even after meeting them in a human body, the rarest of rare could only glean who they are. One has to fulfil the extremely difficult pre-requisites to meet them and have their blessings. There is nothing surprising if our eye-sight fail to catch the presence of great sages in and around Kailas-Manasarovar.

Parikrama of Mount Kailas

For the Kailas-Manasarovar yatris, after leaving behind Taklakot, the next encampment comes after negotiating a distance of 140 km by road at Darchen (Great Flag), which is situated at an altitude of 5,182 metres (17,001 ft.). Important places on the way include Rakshastal, Manasarovar, and the sandy expanse speckled with greenery of the Barkha (Parakha) plains. Beautiful but intermittent glimpses of Gurla-Mandhata mountains and Mount Kailas considerably raise the heart-beat during the journey. The modern highway terminates at this business centre with reasonably good infrastructure and amenities.

Darchen is located south-west of Kailas, almost at its feet. The yearning to see Mount Kailas from a relatively closer range becomes a reality after reaching here. Just behind the Darchen hillock appears Mount Kailas in grandeur as if Lord Shiva, in complete equanimity seated on a big lotus, is immersed in the eternal bliss and ever-ready to bless his devotees. To many, Mount Kailas looks like a dome or a pagoda on the roof of the earth from where Lord Shiva oversees the world.

Glimpses of the abode of Lord Shiva which is the pilgrim's ultimate destination transmit peace as well as energy with humbling effect. The heart and mind are almost overwhelmed with a deep sense of gratitude to the almighty. Thoughts of any adverse climatic conditions, including shortage of oxygen to breathe with full ease, do not cross the mind. In sublime weather conditions, one could see and experience being at the feet of the divine mountain. However, in the event of the weather playing spoilsport, neither Mount Kailas with its shining, bright and beckoning face nor the plains along with the big blue Rakshastal can be seen, despite being in close proximity. Its as though defeat is being snatched from the jaws of victory!

Darchen, this emerging centre of trade and business which in the pre-1959 period used to be an important centre of wool trade, faces the vast amphitheatre-like Barkha plain. It is the starting point for the 52 km (32 miles) long parikrama, the outer kora, of Mount Kailas. 'Kora' is a transliteration of the Tibetan word 'Skor-ra', which means circumambulation or revolution. The steps taken on the kora are meant to move a person along the path to enlightenment for all living beings. With every step until Mount Kailas exuding its spirituality is sighted up-close, the pilgrims carry with them sharp images of the panoramic view seen from the Darchen hillock of Holy Kailas on the one side towards the north and Parakha plains joined by Rakshastal appearing as blue as the sky a bit on the other side to its south. Another view towards the east provides a glimpse of the Gurla-Mandhata at the horizon.

Although Kailas mountain ranges are stated to have expanded from Kashmir to Bhutan, the specific area in between *Lha Chhu* and *Jong Chhu* is what delineates Kailas in practice. There are four other mountain peaks making it a triangle in conjunction with Kailas. Those interested in the parikrama have to go around the group of these mountains.

Three parikrama or kora paths of Mount Kailas are well defined for the Buddhists, each of which is intended to be used by lamas and pilgrims depending upon their spiritual elevation. The outer and the longest one is meant for ordinary human beings, the intermediate one for the dakas and dakinis, and the inner kora for the 500 arahants who had accompanied the Buddha.

There are five monasteries or Gompas in the three koras, although pilgrims on the outer kora would come across only the first three described below. The climate is largely extreme and challenging, with icy-winds that chill every part of the body, the slopes of mountains treacherous in parts with snow-filled crevices and cold slush in some others, rocks with jagged edges that hardly give cushion to rest-a-while, and the air rarefied enough to snatch away breath itself forever. Despite the most basic accommodation and food that could never be stomached by a vegetarian who typically carry their own rations and hire cooks for their parikrama, these monasteries are the most welcome haven after a tough trek. They bring relief and succour to aching legs and feet and chilled-to-the-bone body that no soft-bed in a seven-star hotel could provide.

For the curious pilgrim, the five monasteries hold the inordinate fascination of a rare opportunity of viewing the rarest of ancient treasures in their caverns. The colourful decorations in monasteries lure even the weary traveller to get up after minimum rest to explore the various murals, scriptures, and thangkas (Tibetan Buddhist paintings on cotton cloth and delicate applique work on silk) seen there. There are relics, statues, and sculptures with mysterious and wonderous legends attached to them, which often have the sublime deity jostling with wrathful visages of demons and supernatural beings. Conch shells with an engraved *kalchakra* (कालचक्र), tea-pots that brew blood if touched by the sinner, copper-pots and other religious-cultural items. However, having undergone through years of weathering, all the monasteries with different mystery and legends suffered some damage to different extent.

Foremost, these monasteries that hug the Sacred Soul and the narratives attached to them are reminders of the land on which they exist and what Mount Kailas symbolizes – the co-existence of multiple Gods and Great Masters of various religions living as one Supreme Consciousness since at least 25 million years if the geological calendar of Mount Kailas is contextualised with the mythological calendars of the Deities of Hinduism, Jainism, Buddhism and Boen faiths. To a few it is an adventure, but to the fortunate few every dawn and sunrise at Mount Kailas brings the exquisite emotion of fulfilment and enlightenment.

Nyenry or Chuku Gompa (on the west side), at an elevation of 4,875 metres, is the first monastery on the outer circuit. It is stated to have been established in the thirteenth century by Drigungpalama, it got its name as Chuku

Rinpoche (the Buddha of Boundless Light) monastery. Legend has it that an invading army tried to steal its three objects, the Chuku statue, conch shell, and teapot in the seventeenth century. However, the Gods exert their magic power rendering the statue so heavy that the army abandoned it by the river-side, the conch shell with magic flew back to the monastery, and the tea in the teapot when boiled turned into blood. The invading army went away empty-handed. Dera/Drira-phuk monastery (on the north) at 4,950 metres (16.210 ft.) is where pilgrims take their first night-halt with simple food and quite basic accommodation during the trek along the outer kora. The name Drirapuk in Tibetan language means 'cave of female horn'. As if to create its uniqueness, the name finds reflection in the paintings hung on its walls and the indentations of '*dri's*' (horn) made in its walls. The monastery as seen today was reconstructed in 1986 after the original had been destroyed. Before exploring some of the treasures stored in this monastery, which include the precious statues and historical relics, the further trek right up to the foot of the sheer icy north face of Mount Kailas to pay obeisance (*Charan-sparsh*) is impossible to resist for the trek-hardened and die-hard pilgrim.

Zutrul-phuk (Cave of Miracles) monastery (on the east) at 4,790 metres is reached after crossing over the Dolma-La, and on reaching it only about 11.3 km separate the pilgrim from the finishing point of the outer kora. This is the second night-halt, and the accommodation is less spartan as compared with Drira-phuk monastery. Legend has it that Milarepa and Naro Bon Chung, used their magical powers to make a shelter here, which had their foot and hand imprints on the ceiling of the building and footprints on the roof. The current monastery was rebuilt in 1985. Its natural landscape is also quite breath-taking.

Gengta/Gyangzha/ Gyangdrag (within "calling distance") monastery (on the south) has the highest elevation at 5,075 metres (16,650 ft.). It was established by Ghuya Gangpa at the early thirteenth century as the oldest and most important Drikung monastery in Western Tibet. Ghuya Gangpa organized the spiritual life of his hermits under the supervision of a retreat master (rdor 'dzin) and supervised the spread of the Drikungpa in the region for 25 years. It has a most distinctive architecture, and is said to contain amazing relics, statues and murals. Although by the sixteenth century, the monastery was in a high state of decay, it was practically rebuilt by the then Dorzin and it also attracted the attention of the regent Sangye Gyatso and the 5th Dalai Lama in the seventeenth century. Besides being famous for 33 Vajra holders, the series of Dorzin have continued without interruption until present.

Selung monastery (further south) stands at 5,000 metres, is actually the first monastery to be encountered on the inner circuit. It is stated to have been built about seven hundred years ago for meditation for the monks. It has since been demolished and stands in ruins, and hardly any images are to be seen except for a derelict chorten (chortens which dot the Tibetan landscape are religious monuments which have their origin in the ancient stupas of India). Trekking along the west of Mount Yinjietuo from Selung monastery till the foot of the sacred Mount Kailas, the natural swastika formed by large ice cracks on its south face can be seen in all its glory. The rock-bed traces and white snow on the slopes can also be identified marking the geological time-calendar of its formation in Gangtse range.

Going further ahead, pilgrims who have done the kora around an outlier in the southeast, the Nandi (Neten Yelakzung in Tibetan) at the altitude of 6,000 metres (19,685 ft.), would also find the Saptrishi Caves or 13 golden chortens

(Serdung Chuksum), where relics of former Gyangdrak administrators are said to have been enshrined. Nandi is sacred to the Hindus, as they hold this mountain to be a bull (Nandi in Sanskrit), the riding animal of Lord Shiva. The Buddhists believe the Nandi to be the landing place of the Buddha with 500 Arahants. This inner circuit traverses the adjacent Charok Phurdod La/pass at 5,806 metres (19,049 ft.) between Mount Kailas and Nandi.

Leaving Darchen for the parikrama, for about 4 km the path climbs up over the south-western end of the ridge to reach a stone cairn bedecked with prayer flags. This part of the journey can also be done over a rough road. At this point, the pilgrims are blessed with their first frontal view of Mount Kailas' southern or sapphire/lapis lazuli face. Here is also found a Chaktsal gang, the first of the four prostration points in the parikrama. Lha Chhu Amitabha Western Valley begins from here. From here on, the parikrama enters the Lha Chhu valley and moves alongside the narrow Lha Chhu which has its source in Mount Kailas, all the way to Drira-phuk Monastery about 20 km away.

As the trail now turns north the Yam Dvar (यमद्वार) or Gateway to the God of Death / Salvation comes squarely into view. About 100 metres to its east is a massive flag staff called "Tarboche" flagpole. It is said that the first pole was erected in 1681 during the reign of the fifth Dalai Lama to commemorate a military victory over a part of Ladakh. Yam Dvar and Tarboche are both adorned with thousands of multi-coloured prayer flags fluttering gaily with the winds and scarves arrayed on strings radiating out from their pinnacle. Interestingly, the rectangular pieces of fabric forming the flags are usually arranged in series of five colours–blue, white, red, green and yellow for the five elements sky/space, air, fire, water and earth, respectively. Just to the west of the Tarboche is the Kangnyi Chorten, meaning two-legged chorten, which is decorated with hanging yak heads.

Every year, a big festival of Saga Dawa, which marks the birth, Enlightenment, and death (Nirvana) of Sakyamuni Buddha is held here for two days on Vaishakh Shukla Chaturadashi and Buddha Purnima which falls in the fourth Tibetan month (in May or June). Pilgrims from all over Tibet gather at this sacred Tarboche on the occasion of their festival. On this occasion, the pilgrims ritually replace the flagpole and old prayer flags with new ones. It is believed that if the pole stands absolutely vertical, all is well, but if it leans towards Kailas things are not good and in case it leans away from it, then things are even worse.

As for the Yam Dvar, it is auspicious for a pilgrim to walk through the small chorten archway. The location of the Tarboche is linked to the first of four sky-burial sites (called Drachom Ngagye Deutrto) located a short climb up on a ridge to the east of the Tarboche. The whole of this rocky plateau is revered, including the sky-burial site, and is called the Mandala Terrace of the 84 *maha-siddhas*. Near the sky-burial site is a rock enclosure protecting the first of the three Buddha footprints on this kora, created when the Buddha Chomdende ("The Victorious One") flew here in the company of 500 *arahants*.

According to a local popular legend, pilgrims become free from the fear of death after doing three rounds of Yam Dvar holding a piece of stone, and thereafter by passing through its gateway in order to make an entry into the heavenly abode of Lord Shiva. It is open for all pilgrims. In a real sense the parikrama commences after entering the Yam Dvar and exiting through to the other side. Pilgrims thus get freed from all negative energy generated from past sins. It is widely believed that Yamaraj personally guards this Dvar in pursuance of his promise to Lord Shiva that he would not allow anyone to enter the surroundings of Kailas with negative energy. There is no authoritative year or period of its construction.

After trekking about one kilometre from Yam Dvar, locals with yaks and ponies are seen waiting for pilgrims offering their services. Pilgrims, therefore, have the option of proceeding on foot or to take assistance of a porter and pony/yak. It is desirable to remain careful in dealing with freelancers. While there is some symbolic guidance from the local guide for the official groups of pilgrims from India, those who travel via Kathmandu privately under contract with travel agents are found suffering in the hands of some of them. Some insist on a sizeable advance payment the previous evening. Pilgrims thus run the high risk of the selection pocketing their cash and not showing up the next morning when you need them.

Quite soon the Chuku (Nyenri) Monastery is reached, which is perched high above the valley floor blending almost invisibly into the rocky background of the large mountain. The zig-zag path climbing up to the Gompa takes about 30 minutes, with boulders carved with mani mantra at practically every turn. But the effort is so worth the huffing and puffing. The white marble image of Amitabha Buddha called Chuku Opame (of Infinite Light), which is said to be the oldest and most precious of Kailas, having originated in India. Though the pilgrimage has barely begun, the statue's expression of supreme bliss and enlightenment creates a yearning for the same in my heart. The conch shell is beautifully inlaid with silver, and besides the copper pot were elephant tusks, as informed in conversations with the guides, which had been leftover from when Bhutan exerted religious control over the monasteries around Kailas. It is seen that the Tibetan pilgrims circumambulate this Gompa.

As the pilgrimage marches on beyond the Yam Dvar, the glacial Lha Chhu valley narrows dramatically at Sershong. After cross over to the other side of the river using Chuku Bridge, the valley now recedes simply into the distance between high scree slopes, wonderfully puckered and dented as though with specially chiselled skylines by an artist, on either side. These shapes come to life when the narratives from guides pointing them out reveal strong illusions about their shapes resembling Gods, Goddesses and demi-Gods. Around them quite interesting mythological legends can be heard from fellow travellers and guides. Thus, trekking on for about an hour after crossing Chuku Gompa, to his right the pilgrim observes three mountains said to represent three long-life Buddhas, viz. White Tara (Dolma), Amitayus (Tsepame) and Ushnisha Vijaya (Namgyalma). Between the first two mountains, which are fairly close together, is a slim ribbon-like waterfall, silver against dark rocky backdrop bare of all vegetation, known as the tail of folk-hero King Gesar's horse.

Around here is the second prostration point easily identified from its prayer flags. The backdrop is quite clear and dramatic with a clear view of the west or ruby face of sacred Mount Kailas. Nearby, the second foot-imprint of Buddha is seen clearly (unlike the first one, which was not found). Interestingly, these scree slopes have a squat dome-shaped large outcrop of rock said to be the embodiment of Hanuman, disciple of Lord Ram in the *Ramayana*. The Tibetan's call it the Torma of Padmasambhava (Guru Rinpoche). Its appearance is that of a wing of a huge sweeping arc of rock face.

From Tamdrin Dronkhang, the kora starts to climb and soon enough the pilgrims reach Drira-phuk Gompa with a whole series of white chortens showing the way right to its doorstep. Though this is not one, but many pilgrims are seen prostrating here. The journey from Yam Dvar to Drira-phuk is usually rather smooth if the weather holds good.

Drira-phuk is the second monastery on the parikrama at an elevation of 5,080 metres. Pilgrims revel in the night halt here due to its beauteous location in the hillside providing a direct frontal view of the astonishing north face of Mount Kailas. At first sight in the late afternoon, it appears to be a massive, jet-black slab of granite ornamented with alabaster or snow-white stripes.

As per the legends, Lama Gotsangpa meditated here in the thirteenth century AD, and Buddhists aver that he first discovered the kora route around Kailas. In this he was led to Drirapuk by a yak that turned out to be the lion-faced Goddess Dakini (Khandroma) who guards the Khando Sanglam La. This pass is an alternative route for the parikrama of Mount Kailas. This route leads one to the Kuber valley and Kuber Kund. Unfortunately, the official yatra completely prohibits taking the alternative inner parikrama by crossing over Khandro Sanglam La to Kuber Parvat and Kuber Kund. It is believed that Adiyogi Shiva performs meditation at this place.

As viewed from the monastery, Kailas is flanked here by three mountains (bodhisattvas). To its west is Chakra Dorje or Vajrapani ("thunderbolt in hand"), the wrathful Bodhisattva of Energy. To its east is Jampelyang or Manjushri ("Insight"). Interestingly, its images depict it holding a sword symbolizing discriminative awareness in one hand, and a book in the other which symbolizes a person's mastery over knowledge. Between these two mountains is the third, Chenresig/ Avalokitesvara (embodiment of compassion).

From the monastery, a trek of at least 7 km to the base/ foot of the sacred mountain for darshan is just too tempting to resist, even though it is not a part of the formal itinerary of the official yatra. In fact, it is discouraged by the Indian authorities as well as by the Chinese official guide attached to the group. However, a cooperative relationship between these two authorities and pro-active engagement of the Indian Liaison Officer with the Chinese Guide has many-a-time swung this bonanza for the excited yatris. With half of the day already having been taken up in trekking from Darchen to Drira-phuk, some pilgrims opt to rest and prepare for the next day which entails the toughest trek across the Dolma-La.

This off-route adventure is genuinely worth it, even though it comes with huge risks for those who show the grit for it. Besides high-altitude sickness, acute chill and high winds, and utter fatigue, it is a gruelling climb walking up to the Kangkyam Glacier that descends from the sheer north face of Mount Kailas. There is no clear-cut path and pilgrims draw their bearings simply by keeping Mount Kailas in sight. The trek is alternatively over razor-sharp rocks, jumping over and skirting large boulders and rocks, and stomping through the icy waters of the glacial stream originating from the snows of Mount Kailas. Pilgrims generally stop to pray at an altitude of about 5,335 metres (17,500 ft.). Incidentally, some pilgrims on private tours opt to trek some 10 km instead to the glaciers that are the origin of the river Indus.

Staying true to deeply-ingrained rituals, most of the Hindu pilgrims prefer to remove their shoes and walk the last 50 metres or so just wearing socks to pay their obeisance and touch the "feet" of the sacred mountain, besides doing puja. The whole to-and-fro trek takes about 6 hours, and the return journey is partly undertaken in darkness. The hard grind, topped by touching the God brings a blissful deep sleep to the pilgrims.

Rising before sunrise is a must at Drira-phuk in order to have the mesmerizing darshan of the 'Golden Kailas'. The sensory delight is beyond words. As the sun rises in the east its light reaches the peak of Mount Kailas, which responds by changing its colours to the richest gold. This is nature at its most mystical. The view of the north-face of Mount Kailas is most attractive from Drira-phuk, especially if seen from the rooftop of the monastery. Thus, during the day Kailas presents the brightness of a freshly created palatial mountain for Lord Shiva while at the time of sunrise and sunset, it turns golden taking another divine form. This natural beauty, personified in the form of the Golden Kailas, may not be experienced if the mountain plays a game of hide and seek in the company of clouds for days altogether.

Thus, after the morning darshan, the most difficult stretch of outer kora of Kailas now starts from Drira-phuk. Mount Kailas goes out of sight during the strenuous zigzag climb for the next 3 km reaching up to a plateau at the altitude of 5,200 metres (17,060 ft.) by passing the entrance of the Polung Chhu valley, which runs parallel to Gangjam Chhu valley towards Mount Kailas, when another view to its northeast corner opens.

Pilgrims chant the mantra of *Om Namah Shivaya* (ॐ नमः शिवाय), which sustains them, even as they march ahead slowly in the oxygen-deficit high altitude zone. The craggy mountains delight them, despite the challenging weather, particularly strong winds that whistle loudly, and wind tunnels with gusts of wind threaten to blow them or any loosely held baggage or clothing item. Pilgrims start seeing images of the trident of Lord Shiva, hand claw of Ravana, etc. in naked rocks of different shapes. There is no limit to human imagination. After all, creation as they say depends upon the individual's perception. A line drawn naturally in the centre of the mountain is readily perceived by many persons to be a rope, which in their fertile imagination, might have been used by Ravana to tie Mount Kailas in an attempt to uproot it and carry it with him. Many devotees thus interpret the lines drawn on the southern face of Mount Kailas as stairs carved out by the great King Mandhata in Sata-Yuga for climbing the mountain in connection with the coronation of Lord Shiva. Faithful devotees also find images of Gauri, Kartikeya, Ganesa and their rides in the rocky skyline of the mountain.

From Drira-phuk, the Dolma/Dolma pass is about 7 km. Pilgrims have to navigate a path which twists across a rocky slope, more often than not in foggy conditions.

After trekking past the Jarok Donkhang at 5,290 metres (17,360 ft), but before reaching Dolma La, there is a special place called Shiva Tsal or Vajrayogini Burial Ground, one of the eight great Charnel grounds (Sky burial in Tibetan Buddhism) in the Hindu culture. It is a rocky expanse dotted with stone cairns draped with items of clothing. It is here that pilgrims leave some item of clothing they have worn, a lock of hair, or even a few drops of own blood, which thus get added to the heaps already on the ground, as a symbol of their life before crossing the Dolma La. These offerings are meant to create a physical link between the spirit and this holy site and to prepare the soul for its long journey between this life and the next. It is also informed by the guides that people who die in the kora are given a sky-burial, a holy Tibetan burial, which is different from any other way in the world at the end of a life.

To cross the Dolma La is the option to leave behind past sins and indiscretions and begin a new life. It is akin to a symbolic death, leaving the old life behind. And here, the pilgrim faces Yama, the King of Death, whose judgement purifies him for the next new life awarded atop the Dolma-la. While some actually believe that offerings made at Shiva-Tsal earn the spiritual merit gained by dying on pilgrimage, others believe that they ensure a rebirth in the land of the Buddha. Sometimes monks perform death ceremonies at Shiva-Tsal. The monk chants holy mantras while the pilgrims pretend to be dead. The end of Shiva-Tsal on the trail is marked statedly by a red footprint of Milarepa.

Across the valley from Shiva Tsal, one of the trails provides the pilgrim an option to move towards the inner kora through the tricky alternative of crossing the Khandro Sanglam La, the pass at 5,675 metres (18,619 ft.). As per legend, it is said that a pilgrim can cross the secret path to Khandroma successfully only if he has completed 12 outer koras in his present and past lives prior to this kora.

On the official route, the path after Shiva-Tsal leads to the next plateau at an altitude of 5,400 metres (17,717 ft.) where there are two rocks forming a small tunnel are called the "Sin-testing stone" of Bardo Trang. Tibetan pilgrims try to wriggle through this tunnel, as it is believed that only those succeed whose *karma* is not loaded with sins. This evokes memories of the "garbhajoon" at the Mata Vaishno Devi Temple near Jammu in India. High above the trail is also a large mirror rock; it looks red to ordinary people, white to bodhisattvas, and black to sinners. Further down is yet another even more convoluted passage under the Dikpa Karnak which can be yet another measure of sin-testing by pilgrims who wish to confirm their previous results.

Interestingly, the river-bed of a stream that crosses the trail just short of snow-covered Drolma-La as per one narrative is said to contain tiny black stones which are akin to an antidote or 'pill' swallowed to purify the negative karma of pilgrims that comes from slaughtering animals. Drolma-

La is the highest physical, emotional, and spiritual point at an altitude of about 5,653 metres (18,547 ft.) on the established route for parikrama. Many Tibetan pilgrims perform their prostration here in the direction of the sacred mountain or sit down and whisper prayers. From Dolma-La one could notice another mountain range on the north of Kailas which appears snow-capped. Probably, this is mythological Alaka Puri, home of Kuber, as has also been described by poet Kalidas in his book Meghadutam.

Drolma-La symbolizes Goddess Tara. It is found to be fully covered with prayer flags. The only shape that is clearly discernible and visible beneath all the prayer flags strung together in long and strong strings is the large "Dolma Do" (Rock of Dolma or Goddess Tara). In Tibetan language it is also called Phawang Mebar. Crossing over the Dolma pass represents a transition from former life to a new one with all previous sins forgiven by this compassionate Goddess of Mercy.

The tale associated with the revered Dölma Do is worth recalling. When Götsangpa pioneered the kora and wandered into the valley of Dakini (Khandroma), he was led back to the correct route by 21 wolves that were, of course, merely 21 emanations of Dölma (Tara), the Goddess of mercy and protector of the pass. Reaching the pass, the 21 wolves merged into one and then merged again into the great boulder. To this day Dölma helps worthy pilgrims on the difficult ascent.

Thus, followers of Buddha from across the globe, locals and other pilgrims are found bowing down before 'Drolma Do' in addition to offering colourful pieces of silken clothes or flags as a mark of respect to their Deity. Pilgrims can also be found offering yak butter, pinches of tsampa (Tibetan staple food made from roasted barley/ wheat flour and butter tea), money, portraits of pilgrims, strands of hair, old clothing, human teeth, horned sheep skulls, etc. They are required to leave an object and take one here; the strip of prayer flag offered earlier by someone thus obtained now becomes a lucky amulet for another.

The calm of Drolma pass gets disturbed not infrequently by the sounds of strong winds and thundering clouds. Slippery stones and glacial snows challenge the pilgrim further, compounding his difficulty in breathing with oxygen-deficiency due to the thinned-out atmospheric air. Leg and other body movements become very slow for the same reason. Trekking up to the Drolma pass is indeed the most difficult part of the parikrama.

Despite difficulties in breathing and instructions to swiftly move down to a safer altitude, in case weather permits, Hindu pilgrims are found squatting and reciting mantras and singing bhajans and odes to their beloved Lord Shiva-Goddess Parvati. It is not unusual to find them performing a short 'havan', with all the paraphernalia for lighting a fire in a small havan-kund, dhoop-deepak, etc. having been carried up by them.

For sure, after reaching Drolma pass and finding a taste of the view in the surroundings simply adds up to convert every bit of physical exhaustion that a pilgrim feels into sheer delight. The spiritual satisfaction of having stood as close as possible and even having paid obeisance by touching the "feet" of treasured Kailas is immeasurable. The emotional quotient peaks at the same time but with a multiplicative factor beyond rationality or comprehension.

The onwards physical journey from here is generally less strenuous. Pilgrims tread slowly and cautiously as the steep downward slopes can be tricky and slippery. Using ponies and yaks on this section amounts to risking one's life. Porters are also known to caution pilgrims on foot to remain vigilant and quick-witted as yaks and horses carrying their baggage are also know to slip downwards uncontrollably. The narrow path-ways between mountain rocks and boulders provide little jostling space for man and beast.

Historically not only Tibetans, but Chinese from the whole of China believed in the teachings of Lord Buddha. The Buddhist traditions in Tibet have remained uninterrupted and are still alive, despite the repressions and destructions of the so-called Cultural Revolution and the strong restrictions on adding a Buddhist temple or even a statue in an existing one, militarily enforced by the political establishment of Communist China.

Tibetans continue to worship Goddess Tara which finds extensive mention in their scriptures. In *Chinachar Tantram* (चीनाचार-तन्त्रम्) there is an episodic narrative about the famous Sage Brahmarshi Vashishtha paying a visit to the holy land of *Kamakhya* (कामाख्या) to meditate on Goddess Tara. When he failed to achieve the desired accomplishment, he decided to curse Goddess Tara for his own failure. Goddess Tara understood the impatience of sage Brahmarshi Vashishtha, and to avoid being cursed, appeared before him personally. She told the sage that there is no way other than to follow the methods prescribed in *Chinachar Tantram* to meditate on her, and that only Lord Vishnu in the form of Buddha knew how to please Her. She advised the sage to approach Lord Vishnu to know the method to be followed to achieve Her blessings and to follow that path of meditation. After hearing such words directly from Goddess Tara, sage Vashishtha left the Himalayas and went across the land called Mahachina. There, he could meet Lord Buddha; the incarnation of Lord Vishnu:

ततो गत्वा महाचीने देशे च नरपुंगव।
ददर्श हिमवत्पार्श्वे साधकेश्वरसेवितम्।।

In the good old days, teachings of Lord Buddha guided the Chinese people. When sage Vashishtha found the followers of Buddha with blood-shot eyes due to their high liquor consumption levels required as per the practices of the Buddhist Tantric School, he pondered on the question as to why by appearing in the form of Buddha, Lord Vishnu had deviated from the teachings of Vedas and conducted himself opposite to what is prescribed in the Vedas:

किमिदं क्रियते कर्म विष्णुना बुद्धरूपिणा।
वेदवादविरुद्धोऽयं नाचारः सम्मतो मतः।।

Brahmarshi Vashishtha stirred up with such thoughts suddenly heard an oracle out from nowhere that it was inappropriate for him to be controlled by the thoughts appearing in his mind and that he should follow the path prescribed for the meditation to please Goddess Tara:

.... नैव चिन्तय सुब्रत।
आचारः परमो योगस्तारिणीसाधने मुने।।

Descent from Dolma-la is among boulders. The narrow path steeply zigzags down to the divine emerald lake called Gauri Kund situated at an altitude of 5.608 metres (18,400 feet). The Tibetans call it Tukje Chenpo Tso, the lake of compassion. The lake, substantially snow-covered even in mid-June, has a length of three-fourth of a mile and width of half-a-mile is 84 feet deep. Swami Pranavanand had used his boat called *Janmabhoomi* in August 1946 to ascertain its actual area and depth. He made an in-depth study of Gauri Kund including its formation and behaviour in different seasons. Most of the time during the year, the lake remains covered by a thick layer of ice. Swamiji has mentioned that after many years, he found Gauri Kund in August 1946 without any ice cover, its thick layer of ice having melted completely. Probably, this divine manifestation of nature generously obliged Swamiji to demystify its outer form to satiate his curiosity.

Gauri Kund appears egg-shaped. It is associated with sacredness and purity. Devotees believe that Goddess Parvati comes here regularly to bathe. Glaciers from Mount Kailas feed the lake round the year. As per tradition, the Hindus are supposed to take a ritual bath here, a baptism into their new life. Many people believe that taking bath in this lake leads to elimination of all forms of physical and mental abnormalities. However, in the freezing cold, only the rarest of the rare can muster courage to follow the traditional bathing here. Probably a very few Tibetan Buddhist monks, and God fearing conservative local people and die-hard Hindus take a traditional bath in the bone-chilling waters of Gauri Kund. Pilgrims mostly fill up a couple of bottles of the holy water for ritualistic consumption or bathing in the comfort of their homes. Some pilgrims take the assistance of the local porters in collecting water for them.

On the further steep, slippery and zigzag descent after Gauri Kund which entails crossing snow fields as well, the view ahead is of the peaks on the far side of Lham Chhu Eastern Valley. The peaks to the right are called Tsering Chenga, abode of five sister protectoresses, who were entrusted by Milarepa to guard Kailas.

Providing another opportunity to get rid of any past sins that might still be clinging on to the pilgrim, there is an interesting upright rock in the shape of an axe to be seen on his right on the way down to the eastern valley. Called the 'Axe of Karma', it is said to be the emblem of the King of Death Yamaraj. Some pious pilgrims counter that the axe has lost its power through the mercy of the Saviouress Tara, because mercy is stronger than Karma. They aver that mercy washes away a sinner's past deeds through tears of compassion for all beings who are suffering. Sharing the suffering of others leaves no place for one's own suffering, and finally results in growing beyond one's own little ego.

The parikrama passes another foot-imprint of Milarepa just before reaching the eastern valley on the descent from Dolma La. To the right on this route, a huge rock topped by the kora's third Buddha foot-imprint (*shabjedrakdo*) stands just above at 5,245 metres. About half-way down from Dolma La, the valley seen on the east is the descent route from the Khando Sanglam La which now joins the main outer parikrama. Looking up this valley provides the only glimpses of the Crystal or Eastern Face of Mount Kailas. This is also the third prostration point. Although the climb down now becomes easy along the smaller incline of the Lham Chhu valley, after the next about 6 km Topchen Chhu joins the Lham Chhu from the east, and the river is now called Dzong Chhu (Fortress River).

The third monastery that comes en-route the parikrama now is Zuthul-phuk at an elevation of 4,828 metres (15,840 ft.). Named after a miracle (zuthul) and cave (phuk), this Gompa contains the statues of Shakyamuni and also Padmasambhava (Guru Rinpoche) in the temple to the left of the miracle cave. Many pilgrims are also found praying to the statue of Milarepa seen in the miracle cave.

From the monastery the parikrama follows the river closely for an hour or so, then climbs above the river to enter a narrow canyon. Amazingly, this Eastern Valley here simply explodes in a last display of colour until the Barkha Plains are reached once more. Tibetan's call this place Trangser Trangmar, Gold and red cliffs, a canyon whose walls are splashed and strained with mineral colours, purple, cobalt and rust. Orange boulders appear as if they have tumbled down a blue slope, some steps later the hues are green and purple, red and black. Awesome.

Just before here are several natural rock footprints at Kandrö Tora or Place of Dancing Dakinis. Here the canyon narrows. The holes gouged into cliff walls are not natural, but made by pilgrims looking for holy stones. Prayer flags are lavishly strung across the river. In the far distance the blue waters of lake Rakshastal can be seen again.

Where the route emerges onto the Barkha plain, close to the fourth prostration point (4,700 m) at Dzongdoe, Gurla-Mandhata is again visible in the distance. The parikrama of Mount Kailas that started in the morning from Drira-phuk, after covering a distance of 19 km, culminates at Zong-Zerbu, at an altitude of 3,670 metres (12,040 ft.). The next and final stretch of circumambulation is rather easier. The distance from Zong-Zerbu to Darchen is only 12 km out of which 6 km is motorable.

The parikrama started from Darchen gets concluded at the same place in the forenoon of the third day. Although a bit tiring, it is possible for healthy and fit persons to perform it in a day with vehicular support on motorable stretches.

The circumambulation of Mount Kailas as mentioned earlier covers a distance of 52 km starting from Darchen, a place also introduced as the Valley of Gods. The major part of the Parikrama is through beautiful valleys and rivers/ rivulets originating from Mount Kailas. The circumambulation is performed clock-wise by pilgrims, but counter clock-wise by the Boen ethnic group. Their commitment to faith and respect for the deity of Mount Kailas becomes evident from the fact that they are seen performing circumambulation not by walking but by body-length prostration. It takes about 15 days for them to complete this parikrama. Similar circumambulation of Manasarovar takes them another 28 days. Many Tibetans believe that the desired results are achieved only after performing three or thirteen rounds of the circumambulation.

The parikrama of Mount Kailas is performed to achieve multiple objectives. According to local legends, this exercise gives peace to the souls of those who have demitted their bodies. It is also believed that by performing a round, sins committed in the life are washed fully. By completing ten rounds, those committed between the period of creation and recreation of the world go away. By completing 108 rounds, salvation is achieved in this life itself. Adding complication to this math is that parikramas completed during full moon or in the Tibetan Year of the Horse are more beneficial than ordinary ones. Healthy persons who complete it in a day are called Ningkar. Many resource-rich persons who are unable to undertake this exercise by self, pay remunerations to others for performing them on their behalf to achieve their desired wishes.

The weather in Kailas-Manasarovar region is unpredictable. It can change all of a sudden. Although as in the other parts of the greater Himalayas, heavy downpour, snow storms, etc do not occur in here, but changes in weather due to fog, light rains, hailstorm, strong winds etc can make the journey and stay of pilgrims and explorers difficult. It is quite likely that pilgrims are not able to have a clear view of Mount Kailas for days together due to cloud cover and fog. Discussing the environmental hazards and sudden change in weather conditions, Sage Vyas writes in chapter 143 of *Vana Parva, Mahabharata* about the strong winds which direct hailstorms and rain non-stop over the whole region and from different directions:

ततोऽश्मसहिता धारा संवृण्वन्त्यः समन्ततः।
प्रपेतुरनिशं तत्र शीध्रवात-समीरिताः।।

Sage Vyas makes a clear mention about the sudden change in weather conditions en-route Mount Kailas:

तस्मिन्नुपरते शब्दे वाते च समतां गते।
गते ह्यम्बसि निम्नानी प्रादुर्भूते दिवाकरे।।

The above depiction says that the sound and fury of windy weather vanished in a short time. Movement of air became normal. Rain water from mountains went down the streams. Cloud cover in the sky disappeared and the sun started shining in the bright sky. In this conducive weather, the Pandavas started moving slowly towards Mount Kailas.

Notwithstanding the difficulties and tiredness the parikrama entails, it is full of excitement and curiosity. It is a greatly satisfying experience for devotees of Lord Shiva and others to complete the circuitous trek offering glimpses of Mount Kailas from all the sides. All through the region, there are commonly two kinds of Mani mounds: one is piled by rocks of different sizes and the other is characterized by blocks and pebbles carved with inscriptions and sculptures, which are upbuilt in an undulating line. Mani stones and mani stone mounds almost everywhere, in monasteries, beside villages, crossing, along paths and on mountains. Sometimes they are decorated with sheep and yak horns.

Usually the universal mantra, Om Manipadme Hum, is inscribed on these smooth stone plates, pebbles and rocks. Images of deities and great adepts and sutra texts are also common themes. Followers will drop a piece of Mani stone to the mound every time when they pass a Mani stone mound. That equals to praying or murmuring sutra texts. Thus, the mani mounds are growing taller every year.

Followers of Lord Shiva and Lord Buddha complete the Parikrama chanting mantras of "Om Namah Shivaya' (ॐ नमः शिवाय) and 'Om Padme Hum' (ॐ मणिपद्मे हुम्)

respectively. In different places on the rocks and stones, one finds mention of the second mantra in large letters which is easy to make out as the Tibetan script is quite similar to Devanagari.

The influence of India on Tibetan culture and mythological narratives is impossible to lose sight of regardless of the current political and ideological differences with China which exercises complete control over Tibet and its highly religious-minded people. One should remain extremely careful and focused during the Parikrama to avoid untoward situations. It is better avoided by the elderly and those suffering from asthma, diabetes or hypertensive.

Unforgettable delights during the Parikrama

Charan-Sparsha of Kailas

Golden Mount Kailas at sunrise; from the first rays to full bloom

Khandro Sanglam La: Alternative Parikrama through Kuber Valley.
Source: **Unknown from the Internet-Web**

Reaching the highest point of the Parikrama, Dolma-La

Shiva-Tsal and Dolma-La, the highest point of Parikrama

Gauri Kund, its sources of water; emerald green when snows melt

After the hard trek, the last section is easier

Parikrama of Mount Kailas recalled during the last easy stretch

Forever

Yamaraj's Axe of Karma; A riot of colours - naturally

Circumambulation through body length prostration

The ॐ *and* 'Om Manipadme Hum' *engraved on rocks, forever*

Epilogue

Spiritual and Spirited Indo-Tibetan Ties

Since the mists of time and living memory of the people of the Indo-Tibetan Himalayas and the plateau, two vastly different adjunct geographical units, trade and cultural ties flourished, unhindered by man, topography and climatic conditions, guided through rugged and challenging mountain passes as though seamless, bringing prosperity to the inhabitants.

E.T. Atkinson in the Himalayan Gazetteers traces the antiquity of trade ties between India and Tibet to at least third century BC. Historians have found indisputable, clinching evidences in relation to trade between Tibet and Kumaon and Garhwal regions of Uttarakhand since the sixth century AD. Goods traded by Tibet through the mountain passes in northern India reached as distant as Kolkata and Lahore as per the recorded accounts of eighteenth and nineteenth centuries. The commodities supplied by Tibet included cattle, borax, yak tails, salt, wool, furs, gold, and traditional medicinal products. Indians traded these with woollen clothes, grains, spices, sugar etc.

Other available records, including those maintained by British administrators, show that this trade was an important source of income in what is now Uttarakhand and was carried out through mountain passes including Lipulekh, Darma, Limpia, Kungri Bingri, Uta Dhura, Jayanti, Mana and Niti. Underlining the significance of Indo-Tibetan trade, E.K. Paew in his Settlement Report of 1886 (as quoted by Prof. Ajay Singh Rawat in his Paper- "*Administrative History of British Kumaon*") mentions: "*Tibetan trade offers employment to thousands in the most sterile parts and provides a market for produce in the same region*". C.A. Sherring, Deputy Commissioner, Almora, wrote in 1905 to Secretary, Government, Foreign Department: "*The object of my visit to Tibet was to informally exchange courtesies with the border officials, to report, with the assistance of Thakur Jai Chand, British Trade Agent at Gartok, as to measures required for developing the trade and pilgrimage traffic between United Provinces and Western Tibet and for this purpose to visit Taklakot, Guanema, Manasarovar lake and Kailas, and finally to enquire generally as to the existing obstacles to the development of trade with Taklakot, Guanema and Gartok*".

Pilgrimage traffic and other cultural ties between India and Tibet had been intense is also evident not only from the spread of Buddhism by preachers from India, but also from the fact that sages and seers of this ancient nation found places in and around Kailas-Manasarovar most conducive for pursuit of spirituality, in addition to remote regions in the higher Himalayas.

Indeed, many Indian scholars, including Mohan Lal Babulkar (as mentioned by Prof. Rawat *ibid*) believe that the original Badrinath was in Tholing in Western Tibet. Dr. B.R. Chatterjee is reported to have presented a research paper "*Tholing Math in Western Tibet*" at the Fourth Session of Indian History Congress in 1940 in Lahore to state: "*The Sanyasis say that this (Tholing) was the origin of Badrinath and Shankaracharya ordered the removal of the seat to Badrinath in the Indian side of the Himalaya when he came to realize the difficulties experienced by the Indian pilgrims in their attempt to reach Western Tibet*". In course of his research, Prof. Rawat verified documents maintained by the *Dharmadhikari* (धर्माधिकारी) of Badrinath referring to the '*Dastur*' exchanged between Tholing monastery in Western Tibet and Badrinath shrine since ancient times. Accordingly, the priests of Badrinath used to sent dry fruits to Tholing monastery as token of respect in exchange of musk, saffron and chawar (चवर), (yak tail reverentially waived across the idol during routine rituals). This exchange continued till 1961, when it was stopped abruptly with the unprovoked Chinese aggression against India in 1962. Hardly surprising that Tholing monastery used to be a preferred place in Western Tibet for sages and seers from India.

Large numbers of sages, seers, and pilgrims had been visiting Kailas-Manasarovar through mountain passes of the Himalayas and spending time in the monasteries in past. It stands testimony to the deeply-knit spiritual relationship between India and Tibet. The British administrators could not lose sight of this reality. The Assistant Commissioner, Almora in his letter sent in 1907 to Commissioner, Kumaon mentions: "*At present 150 Faquirs visit to Kailas in an ordinary year. When Kumbh Mela takes place every 12th year, the number of pilgrims from India rises to 400*". The regularity and periodicity remove any doubts of ad hoc and sporadic ties. The further fact remains that the sages, seers and pilgrims would hardly report their movements to the officials or anyone else, as there were no restrictions on their visits across the Himalayas in the good old days. Kailas and Manasarovar were inseparable parts of the respective spiritual journeys of the great Indian masters.

Ancient Indian literature, particularly the segment related to spirituality and mythology is replete with expansive descriptions of Tibet known as Trivitap/ *Trivishtap* (त्रिविटप/ त्रिविष्टप) in Sanskrit and in particular, Kailas and Manasarovar.

Perhaps no other place in India finds such extensive spiritual and literary encomiums and expressions in ancient Indian literature as the holy Himalayas, Kailas and Manasarovar.

In the face of blunt and solid evidences of vibrant and sustained trade, cultural, spiritual and literary exchanges, is ironical that our peace-loving national leadership at Independence took a blinkered view. They lost no time to forget the historical relationship between India and Tibet only to be trapped by the so-called friendly overtures of the expansionist neighbour in the North misleading the vast Indian population with calls of Hindi-Chini bhai-bhai (हिन्दी-चीनी भाई-भाई). India continues to bleed in multiple ways from the thousand cuts, what to speak of the genocide, enslavement and suppression of peace-loving Tibetan people, which was swiftly inflicted after the political brotherly short-sighted embrace by India's visionary leadership immediately after Independence.

Despite these faux political boundary lines drawn in the post-Independence era that sought to extinguish age-old trade and cultural ties between the two ancient neighbours, the fire in the belly and the flame in the mind of a billion-plus Indians to visit Kailas-Manasarovar remain alive. May Lord Shiva dissolve this artificial stressful Chinese Wall between the two contiguous geographical bodies with their common soul.